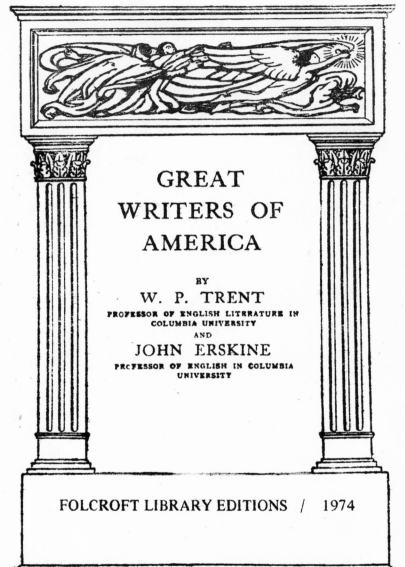

GREAT WRITERS OF AMERICA

BY

W. P. TRENT

PROFESSOR OF ENGLISH LITERATURE IN
COLUMBIA UNIVERSITY

AND

JOHN ERSKINE

PROFESSOR OF ENGLISH IN COLUMBIA
UNIVERSITY

FOLCROFT LIBRARY EDITIONS / 1974

Library of Congress Cataloging in Publication Data

Trent, William Peterfield, 1862-1939.
  Great writers of America.

  Reprint of the 1912 ed. published by Williams and Norgate, London, which was
issued as no. 52 of The Home university library of modern knowledge.
    CONTENTS: Franklin, Brockden, Brown, and Irving. — William Cullen Bryant. —
James Fenimore Cooper. — Nathaniel Hawthorne. [etc.]
    1. American literature — History and criticism. I. Erskine, John, 1879-1951.
II. Title.
PS92.T75 1974   810'.9   74-13032
ISBN 0-8414-8599-2 (lib. bdg.)   Limited 100 Copies

Limited 100 Copies

Manufactured in the United States of America

Folcroft Library Editions
Box 182
Folcroft, Pa. 19032

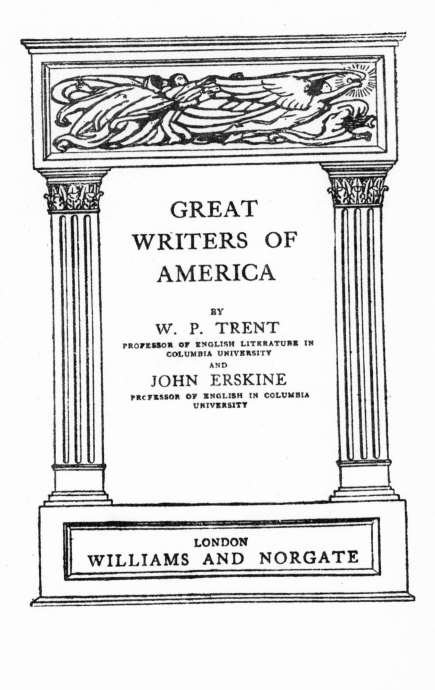

GREAT WRITERS OF AMERICA

BY

W. P. TRENT

PROFESSOR OF ENGLISH LITERATURE IN
COLUMBIA UNIVERSITY

AND

JOHN ERSKINE

PROFESSOR OF ENGLISH IN COLUMBIA
UNIVERSITY

LONDON
WILLIAMS AND NORGATE

PRINTED BY
THE LONDON AND NORWICH PRESS, LIMITED
LONDON AND NORWICH

CONTENTS

GREAT WRITERS OF AMERICA

CHAPTER I

FRANKLIN, BROCKDEN BROWN, AND IRVING

AMERICAN literature in the most liberal
sense of the term is now a little more than
three hundred years old. In the strictest
sense comprising only the books that are still
somewhat widely read, it is not half so old.
Historians may discuss and students may read
or skim a few poets and historians and theo-
logians ; Crèvecœur's *Letters of an American
Farmer* and John Woolman's *Journal* deservedly win an admirer here and there ; a
handful of people know that no American
and few men anywhere ever possessed a more
powerful mind than that of Jonathan Ed-
wards ; but practically only one book written
by an American before the close of the eighteenth century has sufficient excellence and
popularity to rank as a classic. Oddly
enough, this book, Benjamin Franklin's
Autobiography, was first read in an imperfect

French version, won much of its fame in a somewhat emasculated English form, and was not known in its native raciness until 1868. Its author, although his writings fill ten volumes, was far enough from being a professional writer; but his is the first name with which a popular account of the achievements of American men of letters need begin. In the one hundred and twenty-two years that have elapsed since his death the volume of American literature has increased in at least equal proportion with the growth of the country in population and wealth and power; yet among the thousands of authors whose works constitute this literature there is no more interesting and versatile and humane personality than his. The best element in their work, as in his, is a certain " citizen note," a certain adaptability to the intellectual, moral, and æsthetic needs of a large democracy. When this is said, one perceives how it is that one may also say that America has no more produced an author of the range and quality of Dryden than she has produced one of the range and quality of Milton or Shakespeare.

Franklin's life is too well known, too intimately connected with the history of his country and his age, to require extended treatment here. We think of him primarily as a Philadelphian, but his birth at Boston on

January 17, 1706, connects him with that New England which, whether under the domination of the Congregational divines, such as the Mathers, or under the leadership of Emerson and his fellow Transcendentalists, was, until the present generation, the most productive and important literary section of the country. In his shrewdness and his practicality he was worthy of his Puritan birth; not so in his lack of spirituality and his thorough this-worldliness. Perhaps, however, a poetic imagination and a deep religious sense would have made a Franklin of whom the world would have stood in little need—a Franklin far from being the true child of his utilitarian century and the first exponent, on a broad scale, of the spirit of American nationality. He read both Bunyan and Defoe in his youth, but it was the author of the *Essay upon Projects* that chiefly impressed him. He read Addison also, and imitated him in early essays. With such masters and his own native genius, it is not surprising that, given the many occasions he had for putting his pen to use, he should have become the best of the early prose-men of America, a master, like Lincoln after him, of the homely vernacular.

He began his career as apprentice to his brother, who printed the *New England Courant.* He was already in touch with contemporary British literature, already a liberal in

thought, already possessed of practical knowledge of his printer's craft, before he gave his
life one of its few touches of real romance by
running away to Philadelphia and making
his entry, in a rather absurd fashion, before
the eyes of the girl he was afterwards to
marry. Of his first visit to England, of his
subsequent success at home as printer and
bookseller and editor, of his civic spirit,
which made him the foremost citizen of Philadelphia and helped to make Philadelphia itself the foremost town in the colonies, of his
widely read almanacs, of his schemes for
moral betterment and of his services as a pioneer of education, of his scientific experiments
and the cosmopolitan fame they brought
him, of his political activities at home and his
long diplomatic career in England and France
—of all this there is no room and little need
to speak. He was much more than an American, yet always an American, as his proud
independence and his keen, racy humour suffice
to show. He was much more than a mere
provincial, yet his character was in the main
formed amid provincial surroundings. He
excelled, perhaps, in nothing save in versatility
and in a positive genius for the useful and the
practical ; yet it may be doubtful whether any
other name than his is more truly representative of his interesting age. In his writings
that age and the man himself are reflected

with a rare faithfulness, all the rarer, perhaps, because he took so little thought of literary fame, even his *Autobiography* having been designed for his descendants rather than for the world.

Besides the simple, unaffected, fascinating *Autobiography*, which was left incomplete, the general reader will almost certainly enjoy the preface to *Poor Richard's Almanac*, and several of the shorter papers, or occasional trifles, such as the *Rules for Reducing a Great Empire to a Small One, An Edict by the King of Prussia, The Ephemera, Franklin and the Gout*, and the like. Students of history and science, as well as those readers known as omnivorous, will be able to take care of themselves in the vast and varied domain, or wilderness, of print constituted by the *Works*, which are not even yet absolutely complete. One bit of counsel, however, may not be deemed superfluous, even by such experienced readers. It is that Franklin's humour, knowledge of the world, frankness of disposition, and command of a clear, unpedantic style made him one of the best letter-writers of an age supreme in the annals of epistolary literature in English. His private correspondence should be neglected by no one who cares for good letters. But for that matter there is little the wise reader who wishes to know all he can about human nature will neglect in the self-revealing writings of one of the most humane personalities of whom the world has any record. When Franklin died at Philadelphia on April 17, 1790, he closed what still remains, perhaps, the most truly extraordinary and full career, although not the greatest and most inspiring, ever allotted to a citizen of the new world.

The first real American man of letters in the professional sense, Charles Brockden Brown, had not begun his work at the time of Franklin's death. Brown had been preceded by several capable and important writers of the Revolutionary period ; by poets like Trumbull, Barlow, and Freneau, by writers of fiction like Mrs. Rowson,—whose sentimental romance *Charlotte Temple* is still read in unsophisticated circles,—by publicists and historians, but by no writer in whom the public of to-day takes any genuine interest. Even Brown's own novels, fairly eminent follower though he was of Mrs. Radcliffe and Godwin, long since lost the little vogue they once possessed. Yet, whatever his present reputation, it remains clear that the American novel had its serious and its creditable beginning in his books.

Not only do his stories stand chronologically at the beginning of the type, but they illustrate what were to be the qualities of the American novel,—in some aspects, of all American literature. They exhibited, for example, a certain gravity, an exclusive recognition of the seriousness of life, which colours even the romance and is not entirely forgotten in some of the humour of America ; and with his seriousness was bound up an intention to be of service to the community, to explore life and distribute moral ideas for the public good, —the motive of most American prose and verse. This intention precludes in Brown's work any lightness of touch, any naturalness of dialogue, any contemplation—in the philosophical sense—of life. He illustrates also the American avidity for old-world culture ; he imported some of the English radicalism of the late eighteenth century, especially of his master Godwin, some of the French ideas of government, some of the German speculations in mental science and investigations of abnormal psychology. But if he learned from Europe, he also gave something back. He was for a while reckoned greater than Cooper. His books were in every circulating library in England. Their titles were so familiar that Walter Scott, in *Guy Mannering*, named one hero Arthur Mervyn and another Brown. He gave the American landscape and the American Indian their first foothold in popular literature. What is more, his stories are full of American ideas, or, at least, of an American point of view. Shelley, for example, found in this new-world disciple of Godwin something he never found in Godwin himself. Brown's four principal stories, so Peacock tells us, were those which, with Schiller's *Robbers* and Goethe's *Faust*, took the deepest root in Shelley's mind, and had the strongest influence in the formation of his character.

Brown's career was a natural resultant of his temperament and of the times in which he lived. Born in Philadelphia on January 17, 1772, he was close to the American Revolution, and for most of his short life he must have moved in an atmosphere conducive to radical thinking and public service. That his parents were of Quaker descent accounts for some of the quiet of his home; but he was a delicate, thoughtful boy by nature. When his parents wished to walk out on an errand, it was enough to leave him with a book; and he was known to study the map on the wall with such interest as to forget the dinner hour.

His systematic education began in the school of Robert Proud, the historian of Pennsylvania, who taught him Greek and Latin. But, having shortly ruined his health by over-study, he was removed from school and encouraged to take exercise out of doors. In spite of this relaxed programme, by his sixteenth year he had made versions of portions of the book of Job, the Psalms, and Ossian; and he contemplated three epic poems —on the discovery of America, the conquest of Peru, and Cortez's expedition to Mexico.

When his health permitted, Brown was apprenticed to a Philadelphia lawyer, and began to read law. His chief interest, however, was in a more general self-culture; with several other youths he founded a debating society and joined a Belles Lettres Club, and his correspondence shows a most serious, if extravagant, intention to investigate the whole field of knowledge. He had already begun to achieve local reputation as a newspaper poet—though his fame was not always happily arrived at. In August, 1789, the *Columbian Magazine* printed some verses of his on Franklin, in which Philosophy was made to congratulate her son that he had cultivated only the arts of peace; the typesetter by an error substituted the name of Washington throughout. But none of these enterprises was soul-satisfying to a youth of Brown's ambition, and the one thing he was not studying was law; it was therefore natural enough that he should have decided boldly upon a literary career, and accordingly he went to New York, where he thought he might find a larger literary field.

For a while his life in New York was but a continuation of his habits in Philadelphia;

he frequented literary clubs and wrote desultory articles for the newspapers. But his thoughts were busy with the radical ideas then crossing the Atlantic—with the political doctrines, for example, of William Godwin and Mary Wolstonecraft. It is not surprising, therefore, that his first publication, *Alcuin*, in 1797, dealt with the social position of woman, and advocated a very advanced theory of divorce. This brief work, in the form of a rather stilted dialogue, made little impression. But in 1798, when his novel *Wieland, or the Transformation*, appeared, Brown immediately found himself a man of note. He followed up the success with great energy; in the next year he published three more stories, *Ormond, or the Secret Witness*, *Arthur Mervyn*, and *Edgar Huntly*. He is said to have worked at this time on five novels at once, but doubtless much of this work consisted in revising his earlier experiments; it is certain that at least one early unpublished novel, called *Sky Walk*, was reincarnated in several later books.

His first novel, *Wieland*, showed the influence of the so-called Gothic school of romance then fashionable in Europe, but it showed also that he was content with none of the crude or mechanical horrors that sometimes sufficed for that school. He loved mystery, but for him it must be the mystery of science.

That his notions of science were extremely elementary does not greatly matter ; he was a pioneer in the study of psychological terror, breaking ground equally for Poe and for Hawthorne. His stories seem weak when analyzed, but they produce their effect upon the reader by the intellectual seriousness with which even jejune plots are treated. The plot of *Wieland* is the history of an abnormal family, already given to insanity, who are driven to destruction by mysterious voices which they think are from heaven. The voices, however, are produced by a mischievous ventriloquist. Extravagant and weak as this framework is, Brown stretches upon it a terrific panorama of diseased mental states, and suggests in the conduct of the ventriloquist, who acts without a motive, some of the mystery of evil.

Ormond, a less interesting book, is the study of the malign effect of selfishness. The hero is a religious and political radical who falls in love with Constantia Dudley, a sort of modern Griselda. Constantia withstands the wicked designs of her lover until he murders her father and in self-defence she has to kill him. Her character has preserved the story in repute, chiefly because Shelley, as Peacock tells us, particularly admired her, and used her name in the title of one of his poems, *To Constantia Singing*.

B

Arthur Mervyn is a far more important story. It owes much to William Godwin's *Caleb Williams* in its portraiture of a benevolent villain and his victimized servant, but it has great originality of its own. The description of the yellow fever epidemic is now its best remembered episode ; at the time it taught other writers, such as Mrs. Shelley, how to draw such realistic horrors. Brown's family had barely escaped the pestilence in Philadelphia, in 1793 ; five years later he went through a similar epidemic in New York, where his best friend lost his life caring for a stricken foreigner.

Edgar Huntly, the third novel of this prolific year, 1799, is interesting, partly as a study of sleep-walking, and partly as one of the earliest treatments of the Indian in American fiction. The story frankly breaks into two parts. The first half deals with the murder committed by a sleep-walker and the attempt of Edgar Huntly to trace the crime. The second part describes the pursuit of Huntly by the Indians, and his rescue of a beautiful girl, their captive. Brown knew the Indians only from the point of view of the towns ; that is, he thought of them as degraded, rum-drinking ruffians, with a few shreds and patches of lingering pride. His Indians are not entirely unlike the fallen Chingachgook in *The Pioneers*. But even without the romance that Cooper found in the red men, Brown's Indians have the interest of novelty, of figures unfamiliar in literature—so unfamiliar, indeed, that Brown himself does not seem quite at home with them.

These books brought him reputation in America and England. They did not, however, add very much to his income. Their immediate effect in New York was to give him enough prestige to float an unlucky magazine, which survived only a year and a half. In 1801 he returned to Philadelphia and spent the rest of his short life industriously labouring on magazines, with excursions into political pamphleteering as a sort of relief from his hackwork. In 1801 he published *Clara Howard*, a rather weak story, notable now because it portrays a concrete sort of modern woman, as the dialogue *Alcuin* had displayed the theoretical type. In 1804 he married Miss Elizabeth Linn, whose acquaintance he had made in New York, and in the same year he published in England *Jane Talbot*, his last novel. It is in a quieter manner than his early stories of horror; it also indicates a decline of radicalism, for the influence of Godwin upon the hero is spoken of as malign. Two years later the indefatigable worker became editor of the newly founded *American Register*, a successful chronicle of events in America and Europe. He was interested in many other projects, and an English reviewer after his death drew attention to his indomitable energy. But he was already a victim of consumption, and he had little leisure to fight the disease. In 1809 he was persuaded to spend a vacation in New York and New Jersey. In the autumn his strength rapidly failed ; and he died February 22, 1810, shortly after the appearance of the first important book of the earliest American author, who is still read to a considerable extent, and with adequate æsthetic pleasure, Washington Irving.

Irving's career was both fortunate and attractive. He was born on April 3, 1875, in the city of New York, which for a short period succeeded Philadelphia and preceded Boston as the literary centre of the young country. He was of Scotch and English descent, and was brought up in old-world ways amid new-world surroundings—facts which partly account for the charge often made against his writings, that they are British in their warp and woof. He was sickly in childhood and youth, and he received little formal instruction ; but he showed an early literary capacity, and a journey to Europe, undertaken for the sake of his health in 1804, both broadened his field of observation and stimulated his interest in foreign culture. On his return he had a share in an Addisonian miscellany,

Salmagundi, which to American readers of
1806 seemed an achievement of some importance. Then, after the death of his
fiancée had given him a background of tender
sentiment,—he never married,—he produced
his elaborate burlesque *History of New York*,
the reputed author of which, Diedrich Knickerbocker, still enjoys, even after the lapse of a
century, a somewhat green old age. The
book is scarcely a masterpiece of humour which
readers of any nationality whatsoever will
appreciate, but it is well sustained, thoroughly
genial, and worthy of the reputation it has
never lost. That its author's genius was not
of the kind that is known as robust seems
clear from the fact that his next work of any
consequence was not published until a decade
later, when Irving had been for some little
time a resident of England, the partner of his
brothers in a commercial enterprise that
failed.

The Sketch-Book, which was first published
in America, in parts, in 1819, remains, probably, the chief basis of the international fame
which Irving began to win on its appearance.
Rip Van Winkle and *The Legend of Sleepy Hollow* made the beautiful Catskills and the valley
of the Hudson not only the home of romance,
but for Americans, in a sense, classic ground.
With *The Spectre Bridegroom* they justify the
claim that Irving was the father of the

modern short story, perhaps the single literary form in which America may claim pre-
eminence. Much of the sentiment of the
book has lost its flavour, and the eighteenth-
century style appears to some readers to be
sluggish and belated, to be as old-fashioned, in
short, as " Geoffrey Crayon " himself, the com-
piler of the miscellany. Some of the themes
have long ceased to interest ; but the felicity
and charm of the book, considered as a whole,
and the versatility of the author ought to be
as apparent to the latter-day reader as to
Irving's contemporaries. It ought to be
clear also that Irving was not merely a ser-
vile imitator of Goldsmith and other British
writers, but an original kindly humourist and
a sympathetic interpreter of England to Eng-
lishmen. *Bracebridge Hall* continued this
work of interpretation, and, like *The Sketch-
Book*, has not outlived its reputation ; but it
may be doubted whether, as a whole, the
Tales of a Traveller were worthy of their
author. The father of the short story was not
an unfailing master of the form, and was
primarily an essayist rather than a writer of
fiction.

Meanwhile, the well-paid and courted author had left England for the Continent and
had fallen in love with Spain, the romance of
which supplied for some years his not over-
creative imagination with materials on which

to work. His *Life of Columbus* appeared in 1828, *The Conquest of Granada* in 1829, and the Spanish medley or sketch-book known as *The Alhambra* in 1832. All were of genuine though somewhat facile merit, and were of special service to Americans in stimulating their interest in that Old World, from whose culture they had so much to learn. In estimating Irving's place in American literature, as in estimating that of Longfellow, this service as a transmitter of culture should always be borne in mind. To judge them merely from the amount of originality to be discovered in their works is to do them an injustice. It should be remembered, also, that Irving, although not a great historical scholar was, nevertheless, a conscientious historian who was, furthermore, a delightful and practised writer, and that he may thus be fairly placed at the head, in point of time, of that group of eminent historians which constitutes one of the chief glories of American literature. Given his tastes and the youthfulness of America, it would have been surprising if, like Bancroft, he had undertaken a magniloquent history of his native republic; but years of absence had not diminished his patriotism, the history of Spain was connected with that of America, and in his old age Irving became the worthy biographer of Washington.

He was one of the first of the distinguished

American men of letters who have served their country in diplomatic positions. In 1829 he was appointed secretary of legation in London ; then, after several years spent in America, during which he saw something of the far West and gathered materials for three new books, he was appointed in 1842 Minister to Spain. He filled the post acceptably for nearly four years, after which he returned to settle down for the remainder of his life on his estate in the valley of the Hudson, known as Sunnyside. There he supervised an edition of his works, wrote his lives of Mahomet and Goldsmith,—the latter, one of his best performances,—and laboured over his biography of Washington in five volumes. The last-named work, completed shortly before his death, would, of itself, have occupied fully the time of a more robust man. Despite its many shortcomings, some of them due to Irving's own qualities, most of them to the contemporary condition of historical scholarship, it has not been supplanted by any biography of its great subject carried out on an equal scale. It was an achievement worthy to mark the close of the life of the first notable American man of letters able to attain the rank of a classic.

That life covered very nearly the entire period between the Revolution and the Civil War. As we have seen, Irving was born in

1783, two years after Yorktown; he died on November 28, 1859, not two years before the attack on Fort Sumter. When he began to write, America had produced distinguished statesmen and soldiers and divines and scientists, but not a single truly important writer in the domain of pure literature. When he laid down his pen, Cooper and Poe had finished their careers, Bryant was already a venerable figure, Hawthorne had but a few years to live, Emerson and Longfellow, with more than two decades before them, had probably done their best work, Lowell, Holmes, and Whittier were already widely known, Mrs. Stowe was famous and *Uncle Tom's Cabin* had almost accomplished its purpose, Walt Whitman's *Leaves of Grass* had begun to divide readers into hostile camps, and Thoreau, although still more or less obscure, was the great writer we now admire. The so-called Knickerbocker and Transcendentalist periods of American literature had been passed through, the scanty literature of the Old South was almost complete, there were signs that there would soon be a literature of the New West. Amid this rapid evolution, literary, social, political, Irving preserved the poise of English tradition and culture; but he combined with it a certain largeness of sympathies, naïveté of sentiment, and geniality of humour that prevented his countrymen from regarding him as an alien. Latter-day Americans often affect to consider him as practically a component part of British literature ; but their own literature has too few urbane writers to be able to afford to lose Irving. Even if he had written nothing but *Rip Van Winkle*, he would have had to his credit one of the few contributions to the literature of the entire western world that any American has made. But he did much more than this. He was the first to give American literature a good and permanent standing abroad ; he was influential in introducing European culture to Americans ; he was a successful pioneer in the short story, in history, and in biography ; and he left a body of writings a considerable portion of which, after the lapse of some two generations, still possesses vitality.

CHAPTER II

WILLIAM CULLEN BRYANT

IF we were to follow strictly the dates of birth of the chief American authors, the name of Cooper, who was born in 1789, would come immediately after that of Irving. The poet who is the subject of this chapter, the so-called Father of American Poetry, was several years younger than the creator of Leather Stocking, and yet was the latter's senior in such literary fame as the young republic had to give. In treating Bryant, therefore, after Irving and before Cooper, we do no violence to literary history, and we give poetry that precedence over fiction which it held in the eyes of contemporaries of the two men.

For, strange as it may seem to us, our ancestors of the first quarter of the nineteenth century thought a good deal of their poetry, and it had even begun to attract attention in Great Britain. To-day the names represented in early anthologies are in most cases absolutely unknown; and such as have been retained in later anthologies either suggest hopelessly faded reputations or are connected with one or two poems of slight æsthetic value and mild patriotic interest. Philip Freneau, Timothy Dwight, the Boanergic President of Yale College, whose epic, *The Conquest of Canaan*, was favourably reviewed by Cowper, Joseph Hopkinson, author of *Hail, Columbia*, Frances Scott Key, author of *The Star-Spangled Banner*, Washington Allston, the painter-poet and the friend of Coleridge, Samuel Woodworth, the author of *The Bucket*, one of those sentimental effusions in verse dear to the heart of the public and vexatious to the soul of the conscientious anthologist, Richard Henry Dana, Sr., and James Abraham Hillhouse,—high-hung portraits in our national gallery of poets,—Richard Henry Wilde, who once or twice struck a true lyric note—all these sons of Apollo had looked upon their father's face before the rays of that divinity fell upon Bryant's cradle in the little town of Cummington, Massachusetts, November 3, 1794.

The thought of the sun shining upon Bryant's cradle suggests the lines

" There is Bryant, as quiet, as cool, and as dignified,
  As a smooth, silent iceberg, that never is ignified,
  Save when by reflection 'tis kindled o' nights
  With a semblance of flame by the chill Northern
    Lights,"

which some half a century later, in *A Fable for*

Critics, the irreverent Lowell applied to the first "bard" of the nation. Dignity and worth are terms one naturally associates with Bryant both as man and as poet; genial warmth is what one scarcely thinks of predicating, either of his character or of his writings. As much the same thing may be said with justice of Milton and Wordsworth, and as Bryant, in his way, was an individual master of blank verse and a true interpreter of nature, we may conclude that the first distinguished poet of America keeps good company, even if we ourselves, like Lowell, find his companionship a trifle frigid.

"If he stirs you at all, it is just, on my soul,
   Like being stirred up with the very North Pole."

Doubtless many good Americans of 1848 had never felt in reading Bryant the frigidity of which the younger poet, the disciple of Keats rather than of Wordsworth, smilingly complained. Probably not a few exemplary Americans of the present day fail to feel this frigidity, and do feel uncomfortably warm with Byron and Alfred de Musset. These are matters of temperament and training which ought to be considered by the student of the manifestations of taste in a modern democracy.

Bryant was the son of a physician, and was named after the famous Scotch professor of medicine, but he was brought up, as befits a poet, in contact with hills and woods and unsophisticated people, and also with good books, including Wordsworth's *Lyrical Ballads*. His precocious attempts in verse were, perhaps, over-favourably received by his father, who actually published at Boston in 1808 his son's satire on Jefferson's peace-policy. It speaks well for no one that the volume should have reached a second edition the next year. In 1810, the youthful author of *The Embargo* went to college for a short period, and then he began to study law, his heart all the while being set on literature. *Thanatopsis* was written in his seventeenth year, although the passage that makes one remember it, the solemn and sonorous close, was not composed until about ten years later. It was a striking poem for a youth, original despite its indebtedness to Blair's *Grave*, to Cowper, and to Wordsworth. Dr. Bryant was entirely justified in sending it to the new Boston periodical, *The North American Review*, where it appeared in September, 1817. A few months later the same magazine published the stanzas *To a Waterfowl*, and discriminating readers were warranted in believing that a poet of true distinction had begun his career in the new world.

This poet was soon invited to deliver the Phi Beta Kappa poem at Harvard, where he

dealt with *The Ages* in a becoming fashion.
One prefers the Wordsworthian treatment of
The Yellow Violet. Both poems appeared,
with others, in a volume published in 1821,
the year of Cooper's *Spy*. The novel was not
innocent of indebtedness to Scott, the poetry
to half a dozen or more British bards ; but
both novelist and poet were none the less true
Americans with eyes fixed on American nature
and on American men and women. " A
stately moralist in verse " is a formula which
does not altogether suffice to describe Bryant,
but does not fall far short of adequacy. He
could be idyllic, patriotic, sentimental, even
romantic in this or that occasional poem, but
in the main he was from youth to age a moral-
izer in blank verse—both morals and verse
being always sure to gain one's respect and
sometimes worthy to hold one's admiration.

In 1825, Bryant removed to New York,
lured by the establishment of a magazine
which speedily failed. Soon afterwards he
began his more than half-a-century's connection with the *Evening Post*, which became
under him the dignified and important newspaper it has continued to be to the present day.
So absorbed was he by his duties as editor and
as leading citizen that for twenty years or
more his spring of genius, never very copious,
almost ran dry. Still he did not cease to
write verse, and sometimes, as in the famous

lines in *The Battlefield*, beginning " Truth crushed to earth," he wrote to excellent purpose. In 1832 a volume with an introduction by Irving made him known to English readers, and he more than maintained his hold upon his own countrymen by pointing out to them the spacious and grand qualities of American scenery, and by inciting them to a noble national life. As he grew older, he became less active as an editor, but as a sage and bard and as a memorial orator he excited a remarkably widespread and real influence. He was a figure to be venerated, though scarcely to be idolized ; and in one particular he proved himself to be exceptional among poets. Much of his later work in verse shows absolutely no falling off when compared with the best of his youth and of his prime. The *Flood of Years* may contain no passage equal to the close of *Thanatopsis*, but it proves that its author had kept throughout his long life the ideals, not merely of a stoic moralist, but of a high-minded poet. It was altogether in keeping with his career and his character that he should have completed in his old age a meritorious blank-verse translation of Homer, undertaken as a solace against the grief caused by the death of his wife. He himself died on June 12, 1878, from the effects of an accident that occurred immediately after he had delivered an address at the unveiling

of a statue of Mazzini. The Republic had
but just celebrated its centenary. In the
hundred years of its existence it had produced greater poets than Bryant and many
far greater writers of prose, but among its
men of letters there had been no more exemplary and impressive personality. Nearly
half a century later this is still true. His art
is that of the elder poets, and seems old-
fashioned and lacking in colour and delicacy ;
but it has elements of largeness and a validity
of appeal that may well be envied by his successors. Fashions in poetry will come and
go, while men continue to memorize and repeat
the close of *Thanatopsis :*—

> " So live that, when thy summons comes to join
> The innumerable caravan which moves
> To that mysterious realm where each shall take
> His chamber in the silent halls of death,
> Thou go not, like the quarry-slave at night,
> Scourged to his dungeon, but, sustained and soothed
> By an unfaltering trust, approach thy grave
> Like one who wraps the drapery of his couch
> About him, and lies down to pleasant dreams."

And with this sonorous passage they will
probably remember the last stanza of the
apostrophe *To a Waterfowl :*—

> " He who, from zone to zone,
>   Guides through the boundless sky thy certain flight,
> In the long way that I must tread alone
>   Will lead my steps aright."

c

This is not the poetry of sophistication ; it is rather the poetry of a simple age and people not yet intoxicated with their own material power and cut off by an ocean from the complex emotional and intellectual life of the old world. In a sense, Bryant was much less of an Augustan than Holmes, who was born fifteen years after him ; but, while in some respects influenced by the romantic movement, he was on the whole neither the child of his own age nor the belated representative of a by-gone generation. He was a rather aloof and eclectic spirit who with no very great increase of natural endowments might have ranked as a reflective poet almost as high as Wordsworth himself. As it is, his stanzas beginning " O fairest of the rural maids " yields to " Three years she grew," and *A Forest Hymn* cannot vie with the great poem which we call for convenience *Tintern Abbey*. But the hearts of his countrymen throbbed in unison with his when he apostrophized America as the " mother of a mighty race," and many a quiet lover of poetry to-day reads and re-reads with pensive pleasure the five stanzas *To the Fringed Gentian*.

Although a New Englander by birth, training, and temperament, Bryant, from his long residence in New York, is treated as the head of the so-called Knickerbocker group of writers. Most members of the group, for example, James Kirk Paulding, a connection of Irving's by marriage, are almost forgotten. A few poems by Fitz-Greene Halleck (1790-1867) are still remembered, particularly the short sincere elegy beginning

> " Green be the turf above thee,
> Friend of my better days !
> None knew thee but to love thee,
> Nor named thee but to praise."

This elegy was composed in memory of Joseph Rodman Drake (1795-1820), a young physician, whose poems were collected some fifteen years after his premature death. The most important of these productions, *The Culprit Fay*, was a more than creditable " poem of the fancy," as Wordsworth would have labelled it, for so young a poet in a country and an age that had done so little in creative literature ; but it hardly deserved the favour it won from a generation for which Poe had already published, " Helen, thy beauty is to me," and it certainly does not warrant any one in connecting the name of its author with that of Keats.

A glance at the poetry of the entire country prior to the first genuine successes of Long-fellow and Poe shows how completely Bryant dominated the generation of which Irving and Cooper were the chief prose writers. Some of his rivals have already been mentioned, others may be recalled only to be dismissed with a few words of comment, which cannot at best be even mildly eulogistic. The truth is that it was a very uncritical and a bumptiously patriotic generation, which insisted on converting an outrageously large number of geese into swans. Every generation will do this to a certain extent, and every democracy will allow itself special latitude in the matter; but no generation, in any form of society, ought, for the sake of its reputation, to be quite so flagrantly blear-eyed in its selection of poetic swans as the generation which stretched from the War of 1812 to that with Mexico showed itself to be. Think of Mrs. Maria Gowen Brooks and her romantic poem *Zophiel, or the Bride of Seven !* It is a comfort, however, to recall the fact that it was the Poet Laureate of the mother country, no less a person than Robert Southey himself, who gave her the name of " Maria del Occidente," and declared her to be " the most imaginative and impassioned of all poetesses." Even Southey would have hesitated thus to characterize Mrs. Lydia Huntley Sigourney, whose popularity was in direct proportion with the fluidity and the sentimentality of her exemplary muse. Almost equally facile was the poetry of the versatile James Gates Percival, perhaps the most self-conscious of these early poets, unless that honour be reserved for John Neal. Here and there the antholo-

gist rescues a poem or two from these well-
meaning and once admired writers ; but the
reading of their works is a task to which even
the most callous of literary historians resigns
himself with a groan.   Such a student feels inclined to bless the lazy slave-holding South
for its unproductiveness, and also for the fact
that among its few would-be poets are to be
found one or two amateurs in whom some lyric
quality is to be discovered.   One of these
amateurs is a Marylander, Edward Coate
Pinkney, who died in early manhood, before
he had had time to write an epic.   Among his
lyrics there are snatches of real song almost
unmatchable in the more pretentious work
of his contemporaries.   But it is as useless as
it is ungracious to dwell upon the failures of
men and women whose love for literature
was genuine, and whose zeal to manufacture
for their country a body of poetry commensurate with its natural resources was praiseworthy from certain points of view.   To
Bryant alone was a fair measure of success
granted ; let the sleep of his poetic rivals be
troubled by no dreams suggested by the evil
spirit of envy.

CHAPTER III

JAMES FENIMORE COOPER

THE psychological, introspective turn which, as we have seen, Charles Brockden Brown gave to the early American novel, was lost for a while in the development it received at the hands of James Fenimore Cooper. All of Brown that could survive in that virile unreflecting genius was the interest in the Indian, and the truthful portrait of the American landscape. But even for these Cooper went, not to Brown, but to his own experience. With Brown he is linked only by the common patriotic desire to celebrate their country in literature. His boyhood and his active life supplied him with all his materials, so that in his best work he owes practically nothing to any foreign inspiration. When he does deal with foreign themes, or adopt a method or follow an inspiration from overseas, he is rarely happy.

Cooper was born at Burlington, New Jersey, September 15, 1789. His father, Judge William Cooper, was of a Quaker family; his

33

mother, Elizabeth Fenimore, was of Swedish
descent.   He was the eleventh of their twelve
children.   The Judge had bought a large
estate in New York, on Otsego Lake, and
there he removed in 1790, and devoted himself to colonizing the country.   What his
occupation was, and incidentally his aggres-
sive personality and his innate literary gift,
are all amply disclosed in a series of letters
he wrote, and had published in Dublin, to
encourage emigration to his lands.   Perhaps
only a hardy soul would care to attempt
the rough life he describes ; his first settlers,
he writes, forgot to plant their crops a season
before they brought their households, and the
settlement would have starved had it not
been for a providential shoal of salmon in
the river.   In this settlement the less reputable element of society, or at least the un-
conventional element, set the tone in spite
of Judge Cooper's effort to rule his domain
with old-world decorum, it was at best a
frontier town.   The faithful portrait of it,
even of the Judge's house, is in *The Pioneers.*

In this settlement Cooper spent his boyhood, until his father sent him to study under
the rector of St. Peter's Church, Albany.
After a brief preparation he entered the class
of 1806, in Yale College, when he was only
thirteen years old.   Whether he had been
precocious in his studies cannot now be dis-

covered, for the college soon dismissed him
for doing no studying at all ; and after some
delay he shipped for a year's voyage on the
Sterling, a merchant vessel bound for England
and Spain. On his return he entered the
navy and received his commission as midship-
man January 1, 1808.   In his first year of service he helped to build a brig of sixteen guns on
Lake Ontario ; in 1809 he had command, for
a short time, of the gunboats on Lake Cham-
plain ; in 1810 he served on the *Wasp* under
Lawrence, the future hero of the *Chesapeake*.
But his naval career ended abruptly when, on
January 1, 1811, he married and settled in
Scarsdale, Westchester, New York State.

Desultory as Cooper's life had been up to
this time, his changes of location had edu-
cated him in almost all the scenes of his
greatest stories ; he was familiar with the
frontier, with the sea, with the great inland
lakes, with the New York and New England
forests. His Westchester residence was to
give him a setting for his first great book. In
1820 a very poor English novel which he was
trying to read, inspired in him a confidence
that he could write as good a book himself.
It has never been determined whether *Pre-
caution*, the result of this confidence, was as
good as the English book, but in this 'pren-
tice writing he discovered his ambition. In
December, 1821, he published *The Spy*, in

New York ; and its immediate success urged him on to write *The Pioneers*, which in 1823 made a similar success. *The Pilot* followed in 1824, with no failing of power ; then, in 1825, Cooper tried to write an historical picture of Boston in the Revolution. As he knew little of the scene of his story, *Lionel Lincoln* was sadly lacking in the magic of the other books. In 1826, he returned to his true field in *The Last of the Mohicans*, by many readers considered his masterpiece. After this astonishing output within five years, Cooper went abroad for rest and study, and did not return until November, 1833.

His literary work in these first years was his best, if we may arbitrarily include with it *The Prairie*, 1827, written abroad, and *The Pathfinder*, 1841, written after his return. This inclusion of later with earlier work is, however, not so very arbitrary, after all, if we remember that in the early period Cooper invented Leatherstocking, and plotted out his life ; the three additional stories in the series were simply delayed in execution. In imagination and in temper they are like nothing else that Cooper wrote after sailing for Europe in June, 1826. It is, perhaps, well, therefore, to think of this early work by itself.

Most of Cooper's quality as a story-teller is represented in *The Spy*, although his characteristic scene is not in that book. He imagined a plot in terms of conflict—not primarily a conflict of ideas or of civilization, though some such spiritual crisis often stands behind his story and ennobles it, but an elemental conflict of strong men fighting for life. He had a singular gift for developing in stories of civilization situations that are motived by the instinct for self-preservation. This conflict he usually imagines in a chase or pursuit. In *The Spy* the two pursuits of Harvey Birch are the central interest; and the whole book reflects the running fight between the two sides, not only in the stir of the action, but in the unusual characters, which are such as flourish only in critical moments. Cooper's feeling for settled society is always strong; he differs from other chroniclers of the frontier in the care with which he insists upon normal standards of civilization; in *The Spy* the Tory family and Washington himself are felt to be the product of desirable order. But along with them, in the upheaval of war, are set such frontier types as Lawton, the Skinner, Harvey Birch —types who would not have a career at all on the Westchester scene, if that scene were not suddenly reduced to a frontier condition.

Harvey Birch in a fashion reminds us of those ultra-romantic heroes in Byron and Scott who stand outside the main stream of life, doomed and lonely, yet are the most

interesting persons in the story. Leatherstocking, Long Tom Coffin, and Paul Jones
are similarly ultra-romantic.   It is misleading,
however, to ascribe this type in Cooper or in
Scott to literary origins ; they each found it
on a frontier, Scott by tradition and Cooper
with his own eyes.   Moreover, Cooper's
ultra-romantic hero differs from Scott's in
being not very heroic after all ;   at least,
Harvey Birch is without distinction, possessed of moral but not physical courage, and
the other heroes have very strict limitations ;
they are American, if not local, and the
glamour of romance is not on them.   Cooper's
indebtedness to Scott in his first novel must
be acknowledged in less subtle matters—for
example, in the device by which Wharton's
coloured servant took his place in the camp
jail, as Wamba took the place of Cedric in
Ivanhoe.

Cooper's best stories usually have an ultra-
romantic heroine, like Miss Singleton in *The
Spy*, who by some pathetic circumstance is
cut off from a normal destiny.   He also portrays in his best tales a very normal hero and
heroine, admirable but not remarkable, who
fall in love and achieve happiness, and help
to assure us of the permanent sanity of life.
Like Scott and Thackeray, Cooper does not
overrate sheer intellect or genius ; happiness
he reserves for the average man.   Indeed, he

usually bestows the shrewdest intellect upon his villains, of whom there is one in every story. The capacity of mankind to be villainous was a capital tenet in his creed. The example in *The Spy* is the Skinner, who in the last chapters is hanged, to the reader's satisfaction. Although this book gives no historical panorama, it is in effect an historical novel, and the portrait of Washington is perhaps its chief glory. From it we derive not only a record of the early idealization of Washington, but indirectly a statement of Cooper's standard of citizenship, which was to bring him before the public later in less pleasant ways.

The Pilot was written upon a roundabout suggestion from Scott; that is, a discussion of the ignorance of seamanship in *The Pirate* prompted Cooper to illustrate the sailor's true point of view. For that reason he laid the plot just off shore, where a ship is in greatest danger; and the story largely turns upon the seaman's preference for deep water, especially in a storm. This setting of the plot provides contrasts between scenes on land and on sea, and gives Cooper the greatest number of chases or pursuits—the kind of episode he excelled in. The frigate among the shoals, the wreck of the *Ariel*, the running fight with the British man-of-war—these glimpses of the sailor's life are not surpassed in fiction.

The story has the usual complement of

Cooper characters,—the lovers, the villain, the ultra-romantic types. The interest, however, is divided by two persons, Paul Jones and Long Tom. The latter is a sort of Leatherstocking at sea—a product of the New England coast, as Leatherstocking is of the New York forest, fatalistic, unpoetical, capable, and lonely. The reader has difficulty in thinking of Long Tom apart from the land version of his type, and perhaps Cooper could not dissociate them ; the final impression is that Long Tom is out of keeping with his surroundings, and as Leatherstocking is always in keeping with his, the deduction, however unwarranted, is that Cooper in *The Pilot* arbitrarily sent his greatest character to sea.

Paul Jones is the most romantic person in the book. Something of the Byronic mood is in his mysterious comings and goings, his theatrical posings in moments of danger, his extreme egotism. He belongs as perfectly to the wild scene of the story as Long Tom seems foreign to it ; and it is evidence of Cooper's literary tact that the mysterious pilot is left on the strange coast where first he was found. We are not convinced that Paul Jones really cherishes the passion that Cooper credits him with ; at least Alice Dunscombe seems no proper inspiration for such a genius. His moodiness is not from blighted love, but from some essential melancholy, of a kind that Cooper never drew so sentimentally again.

In spite of the many great qualities of these two stories, however, it is on the series of Leatherstocking Tales that Cooper's fame rests. Not only is Leatherstocking his one important contribution to world fiction, but the description of the moving frontier, from novel to novel, is majestic beyond anything else in American literature. In its motion this frontier differed radically from Scott's stationary and historic border. The tide of new-world civilization sweeping westward presented fresh aspects at every stage, and its breaking wave could never repeat the journey. In his record of it Cooper seized the most epic of American moments, a climax of destiny; and to no follower of his was the material available for a second account.

Probably no imitator would have approached his use of the opportunity, for he had a very unusual gift—somewhat akin to his skill in describing a chase—of reproducing a changing scene and an aging character. Deerslayer becomes Hawk-eye, then the Pathfinder, then Leatherstocking, then the Trapper; and in the changes he is always the same character, simply growing old. He is accompanied in his aging by a parallel waste of the primitive forest, as though he were a kind of wood god, or at least in some more than poetic sense brother to the trees. In *The Deerslayer* and *The Last of the Mohicans* the forest is primitive : in *The Pathfinder* it begins to be broken with the settlements ; in *The Pioneers* the cutting of lumber is a cause of real pain to the old hunter ; and in *The Prairie* the trees have disappeared, and the tree-lover dies on the plains.

The development of Leatherstocking's character is the more extraordinary because Cooper, who is not usually considered a literary artist, has kept the portrait so consistently true. The young hunter from the Delaware settlements is curiously simple. He has no learning, nor much intellectual curiosity. Strangely enough, although created by one of the most politically ardent of Americans, he has no political nor even social interests,—he is lonely as the forest tree, and pure-hearted as a child. Yet Cooper intends him to represent no ideal primitive man, such as would have pleased a Rousseau or a Chateaubriand. Leatherstocking has almost a colloquial reality. Even his skill with the rifle is liable to occasional lapses, and the Indians outdo him in woodcraft. His chief American trait, which he conspicuously shares with Long Tom, is his fatalism ; in the virgin world he reads the decree of civilization and resigns himself to it, although to him it is in no respect a welcome prophecy.

In Leatherstocking is incorporated Cooper's great love of the woods. This incarnation is often overlooked by readers to whom the Indian is more obviously the child of the forest. The red men Cooper habitually endow with skill in scouting and trailing, as though they had some extra animal sense; but they are nowhere represented as conscious lovers of nature. It needs only careful reading to see that they do not even figure as heroes in these stories; so conscientiously does Cooper refrain from idealizing them that he shows their treachery and cruelty, their lust for revenge and their dulness of feeling, even while he delights in their courage. And the great chief, the father of Uncas, dies a drunkard in the settlements. Yet this much truth is in the familiar criticism of Cooper's Indians, that, though he may not idealize them, his readers do, the world over.

The best story of the series, perhaps the best he wrote, is *The Last of the Mohicans*. The fact that both Leatherstocking and his Indian comrades are here seen at their best, and that the plot represents two long forest chases, with only a slight interim, and with infinite opportunity for the craft of the trail, explains the power of the book. Yet two other stories, the first and last of the series, are more poetic. *The Deerslayer* not only introduces us to the young hunter before he has ever killed a man, or has ever seen an inland lake, but it brings him face to face with Judith Hutter, the most interesting woman Cooper drew. Of his other heroines there are no enthusiastic admirers; but Judith Hutter is a kind of apparition of the civilization which Leatherstocking rejects, crossing his fate at the moment when he might make a different choice. That her past is dishonourable seems a proper barrier between her and the youth to whom purity is above all other virtues; but probably no reader ever closed the book without a sentiment of regret, into which the whole scene of the lake and the dwellers on it is gathered. In *The Prairie*, the poetic element is grand rather than sentimental; all things in the book are large, from the great horizon sweeps to the giant sons of the squatter, Ishmael Bush. This setting does not seem too vast for the soul of Leatherstocking in his declining years. The pictorial quality of this story has not received generally the praise it deserves, nor has Cooper received sufficient recognition for the elemental power which makes this one story so unlike any writing with which his tales are usually compared.

From the time that Cooper went abroad he seemed governed by some perverse fate that rendered his conduct as well as his work tactless and unfortunate. He lost popularity

D

on the Continent by his somewhat vigorous Americanism and he managed to incur the dislike of his countrymen by some well meant but unsolicited discussion as to the relative merits of French and American taxation. That he was only supporting General Lafayette, who had praised the government of the United States, did not count with those whom he had irritated. When he returned to his country, therefore, he had expressed his general attitude toward old-world institutions in three not very important stories, *The Bravo*, 1831, *The Heidenmauer*, 1832, and *The Headsman*, 1833; and he had laid the foundation of much ill-will towards himself at home. This ill-will soon precipitated itself in a quarrel with his neighbours at Cooperstown over a piece of land which his father had left him. Criticism of him spread recklessly in the newspapers, and he soon had excellent grounds for libel suits. From 1837 to 1842 he was engaged in the unamiable task of prosecuting editors either on these grounds or because of attacks upon his history of the United States Navy, 1839. That he won almost all the cases, and that he was legally in the right throughout, did not render him more lovable to his critics, and the quarrels tainted his mind, so that all his later books were controversial and otherwise inferior. The great fame of his best stories, however, steadily increased throughout the world, and his last years were happy in the returning consciousness of America's pride in him.   He died at Cooperstown, September 14, 1851.

Although America produced many novelists during the thirty years of Cooper's literary life,—Dr. Robert M. Bird, Charles Fenno Hoffman, Miss Catherine Maria Sedgwick, for example,—his chief disciple and the only writer to whom, besides Herman Melville, we need devote a few words here was the best known of Southern novelists, William Gilmore Simms.   He was the son of a brilliant and irresponsible Irishman who settled in Charleston, South Carolina, just after the Revolution, and there married Miss Harriet Ann Augusta Singleton.   William Gilmore, the second child, was born in Charleston, April 17, 1806.   Two years later his mother died, and the erratic father, having become a bankrupt, suddenly disappeared into the Tennessee wilderness.

The boy was cared for by his maternal grandmother, Mrs. Gates, who brought him up most wisely, storing his head with tales of wholesome adventure and legends of the Revolution, until his imagination was completely fired.   Less romantically he was in time apprenticed as a drug clerk, with the general idea of studying medicine, but when

his term was up he entered a law office.
Meanwhile his astounding father had returned and had tried to kidnap him, apparently thinking that the grandmother would
not otherwise surrender the child ; but Mrs.
Gates had taught the son to think well of the
runaway father, and now she invited the
elder Simms to make them a visit, in 1816 or
1817. Such stories he told of the Cherokees
and the Creeks that William Gilmore had to
make a journey to Mississippi with his father
in 1824 or 1825, as a sort of climax to his boyhood's romantic dreams of the Southern
frontier.

Not until 1827 was he admitted to the
bar, and on October 19, 1826, he was married.
From 1827 he continually published volumes
of poetry, convinced that his career lay
in that field ; he also ventured into journalism, and in the exciting politics of the
time he took a firm stand and made enemies.
In 1831 a torch-light procession of his opponents almost mobbed him in front of the
office of the paper in which he had part
ownership. The following year his partner
died, the paper failed, and he went into bank-
ruptcy. In this year also his wife died. His
father and Mrs. Gates were already dead.
The tragic accidents of his much troubled life
had begun.

With every reason for desiring a change of

scene, Simms was persuaded to seek his literary fortunes in the North, and he accordingly visited Massachusetts.   He made his first appearance with a long poem, and followed it by an unimportant story, *Martin Faber*, 1833, which yet had success enough to encourage him.   The next year he published the first of his border romances, *Guy Rivers*, and immediately afterward wrote and published *The Yemassee*, his well-known Indian story. That the book owed something to Cooper was at once apparent ; the Indian family in it can hardly escape comparison with Chingachgook and Hist and Uncas. But the comparison is not greatly to Simms's disadvantage. His genius was less simple than Cooper's ; he liked a wild abandon of adventure for its own sake, and in the welter of events the characters, in some of his books, have to look out for themselves ; but in *The Yemassee* the Southern Indians are realistically drawn, and form an indispensable complement to Cooper's picture of the Northern tribes. The historical background of the story is, artistically speaking, negligible.

In 1835, *The Partisan* was published, the first of Simms's important series of novels on Revolutionary conditions in South Carolina. *Katherine Walton*, 1851, and *Woodcraft*, 1852, are other parts of the one panorama which deals with the war and the unsettled condition afterwards, much as Cooper's great series deals with the frontier. As a plot-maker Simms always outdoes Cooper, but his invention is too luxuriant for its own good ; the series of stories seem increasingly formless to the modern reader, although Hurricane Nell, in *Eutaw*, 1856, and Lieutenant Porgy, in *Woodcraft*, could not easily be spared from the few important characters in American fiction, and some of the individual scenes are tragically powerful.

The success of his writings, which included some books now hardly worth recording, brought to Simms the happiest period of his life. In 1836 he had married Miss Chevilette Roach, of Barnwell, South Carolina, and her estate of Woodlands soon became famous as his home. Here he entertained his friends with something of Scott's feudal hospitality, working the while on his books. Fortune was making of him a typical Southern man of property, as well as the leading Southern man of letters ; his condition of life was placing him where he would become a natural champion of the South against the North in the approaching struggle. He accepted the obligations of his position, and spoke out as honestly and uncompromisingly for slavery as Mrs. Stowe had spoken against it. He bore this witness to his cause in Southern journals, where he published much miscellaneous writing.

When the war-cloud broke, however, Simms suffered more than his share of ill fortune. In 1860, as though by way of omen, his house in Charleston was burned down. In 1861 two of his children died of fever, and the next year the larger part of his house at Woodlands was destroyed by fire. His wife died in 1863. He was in Columbia during the sacking of the city by Sherman's troops, and the rest of Woodlands was burned either by the same troops or by negroes. Simms bore each successive blow with fortitude. He made a bare living by journalistic work, and supplemented his earnings by selling his historical and autograph collections. He even partially rebuilt Woodlands and began to write more stories, but his health suddenly broke under the long strain. He died at Charleston, June 11, 1870.

It was in the fertility and excitement of his plots that Simms excelled Cooper, and in this phase of the development of the American novel he in turn is rivalled by the friend of Hawthorne, Herman Melville, born in New York, August 1, 1819. Of an excellent family much honoured for its patriotism, Melville early showed his preference for a roving life, took to the sea, and for some years picked up what education could be got from rough sailing in various parts of the world. This period of his life had its climax on one of the Marquesas islands, when he was captured by cannibals and with difficulty rescued. He turned the experience to account in his first story, *Typee : a Peep at Polynesian Life during a Four Months' Residence in a Valley of the Marquesas*, 1846.

The success of this novel brought Melville back into a more settled life. After some residence at Pittsfield, Massachusetts, he returned to New York and accepted an office in the Custom House. Of his other stories, the best are *Omoo : a Narrative of Adventures in the South Seas*, 1847, and *Moby Dick, or the White Whale*, 1851. This last is his masterpiece. Not even Cooper could surpass the grandeur of its sea-pictures, and some of its adventurous episodes have an uncanny quality found nowhere else. Melville could not repeat this success, nor again approach it. He died in New York, September 28, 1891.

The work of Simms, for its extent and its contemporary importance, is far more worthy of attention than all of Melville's writing, with the one exception of *Moby Dick ;* and the character of Simms was most engaging. But the Southerner's novels are now hardly known by name, whereas the praise of Stevenson and some other craftsmen near at hand has given Melville's best work a new lease of life.   Yet above them both Cooper still keeps his secure place, not much injured by unsympathetic modern criticism, nor even by some condescending praise.

CHAPTER IV

NATHANIEL HAWTHORNE, the next great master of American fiction, was born in Salem, Massachusetts, July 4, 1804, the son of Nathaniel Hawthorne and Elizabeth Clarke Manning. The father was a sea captain, like others of his sturdy ancestry ; the mother was the daughter of a house as sturdy, also English in extraction. It was from his mother that the boy was to take his deepest imprint of character, for his father died in 1808. From that time until her death Madam Hawthorne lived secluded, never eating a meal with her family, and shutting herself up in her room. An older and a younger sister were Nathaniel's playmates.

From the fall of 1818 to the summer of 1819, the family lived at Raymond, Maine, where the grandfather Manning had bought large tracts, and where a house was erected for the widow and her children by Robert Manning her brother. Here the boy got his knowledge of the woods, and was confirmed in those habits of loneliness which, indeed, his home life anywhere would have bred in him.

He had acquired a love of books even before leaving Salem, and now in 1819 upon his return for two years of preparation for college, it was in the love of books that he chiefly prepared himself. When he entered Bowdoin College, in the summer of 1821, he must have been one of the best read students, if we may judge from his letters to his mother and his sisters. But Longfellow was a classmate of his, and clearly outshone him in study; Franklin Pierce, afterwards President, was his best friend in the class ahead of him; and even without those rivals Hawthorne would not have excelled as a scholar. He was rather given to recklessness, and barely escaped getting into serious trouble, along with others of his set, for card-playing.

Upon his return to Salem Hawthorne drifted into his literary career, rather for lack of something else to do than for any purpose. At least that is the impression which he himself gives us. But the patience with which he now began and continued to practise and perfect his art, even though he had no public, indicates some guiding motive. His first publication was *Fanshawe*, a short novel, printed in Boston in 1828 at his own expense. The story was the work of an amateur and, apart from some merits which would not be unexpected in any cultured writing, it had no claim to general attention. Some emphasis has been laid upon the fact that it is a story of New England life in a college town ; Hawthorne was drawing the picture of his own country, perhaps of his own life. In view of the native strain in his later writing, it is natural to look for some significance of prophecy in this early coincidence, but, indeed, any young writer would be likely to begin more or less autobiographically. Hawthorne's real genius found its significant beginning in the contributions he now made to various magazines and annuals—contributions often unsigned, or over a pseudonym. The annual most friendly to him was *The Token*, edited by " Peter Parley," S. G. Goodrich. To this publication Hawthorne contributed *Roger Malvin's Burial*, *The Gentle Boy*, and other stories. In *The New England Magazine* also his work regularly found a welcome. But he made no real reputation, and in money he was scantily paid. Through the kind offices of Goodrich he was engaged by a Boston firm as editor of an ambitious project, *The American Magazine of Useful and Entertaining Knowledge.* His salary was to be five hundred dollars (£100). But he had hardly got the magazine started, in 1836, when the publishers failed, and the engagement proved to be for him nothing more than an annoying loss of time and energy.   Perhaps by way of comfort, Goodrich engaged Hawthorne with his sister Elizabeth to write one of the Peter Parley books,—a geographical history or a historical geography,—for which, although the book sold well, the authors received only a hundred dollars.

However unsuccessful Hawthorne had been, he had at least impressed his intimate friends with an enduring faith in his ability.   It was his old college mate Horatio Bridge who now thought of a way to make Hawthorne's genius known to the world.   Convinced that the various sketches would appeal to a wide public if once they were brought together in a presentable volume, he made an arrangement through Goodrich, without Hawthorne's knowledge, with a Boston publisher, whereby he guaranteed the cost of the volume, the profits of which were to go to the author.   Under these auspices *Twice Told Tales* appeared in 1837.

For a time this book made no unusual impression, in spite of Longfellow's hearty praise in *The North American Review* ; but after a year or so it began to take the place it now holds, as one of the most important volumes in American literature.   The critic, now looking back, perceives that in this collection were the germs of Hawthorne's later stories. Three types of writing can be distinguished, which proved to be preliminary sketches for his three best novels.

The first type is the dramatic scene dealing with history, of which *The Gray Champion* or *Howe's Masquerade* are ready examples. Hawthorne selects a critical moment of history, when the new age is in some fashion to overturn the past, and he renders the moment dramatic to the eye. That is, he groups his characters and focuses his scene as though he were setting a stage or a tableau, and the result is an interpretation of history; yet his interpretation gives a totally different impression from Scott's, for example, or Charles Reade's. Clear as it is to the eye, it suggests spiritual mystery. The scene does not stop with romance, nor with the mere memory of the past, but directs attention to a moral progress, an evolution of national or racial spirit, which looks more to the future than to the past. In this sense Hawthorne is in all his work profoundly radical. It is a matter for wonder that conservative criticism has not generally discerned his antagonism to all conventional opinion. Perhaps his significance is, for such critics, obscured by his way of giving to the past a moral purpose, even while he is turning to the future. He likes to in-

corporate the past in some person or symbol
—in the Gray Champion himself, or in the
portrait of Edward Randolph, or in the
Masquerade that startled Howe ; and this
incarnation he makes the herald of some new
order. The paradox is less than it seems.
For it is not the conventional past that is
incarnated, but some profound human dream,
most often the desire of liberty, which the
conventional past has thwarted. Hawthorne's
radicalism, like other radicalism, is but
the persistence of an unaccomplished ideal.

Quite as important as the stories with
historical background are the essay sketches,
like *The Rill from the Town Pump*, or *David
Swan*. Not only does Hawthorne here abandon
the large interest of the historical crisis,
but he portrays no crisis at all. These
sketches have none of that problem-working
that makes a plot. They are in effect meditations upon life. The reader assumes with
the author a passive attitude—imagines himself to be the toll-gatherer, or to be mounted
on the church steeple, or to be turned into
the town pump ; and he then submits to
the experiences that appear from those
points of view. These compositions are not
in the ordinary sense stories, yet like Addison's papers, or Irving's, they are something more than essays. They resemble
Addison's writing or Irving's in this, also,

that their mood is invariably cheerful and sane. Herein they contrast with the melancholy of Hawthorne's other work. But even from the Addisonian or Irvingesque paper they differ, for they convey a profound significance of life, a sense of the human destiny, quite as much as do the historical tales. The inexorable ideals of the race, which in the studies of history appear clothed as the heralds of the future in the dress of the past, are in these sketches expressed by a general sense of a diffused past, an authentic destiny, which might be called, with a pleasant meaning, fatalism.

If so large a word as philosophy may be applied to the significance of life which Hawthorne presents in these essay-tales, it is easy to make their connection with those psychological studies which form the third division of his work. A good illustration is *Wakefield*, the account of a man who for a whim absented himself from his home, and found that fate blocked his will to return; or *Dr. Heidegger's Experiment*, in which are studied half-a-dozen old people who for an hour are rejuvenated by a fountain of youth. In these psychological studies, as in the historical scenes and the sketches, the sense of an ordered purpose in life is strong. But their significance is, on the whole, melancholy; they speak none of the sunny trust of the essay-tales. They suggest that any tampering with life's order is tragic. They announce, with various embellishments of the theme, that he who, for a whim or for other cause, steps out of his appointed place, will find it difficult or impossible to resume his fate.

Fine as are the historical stories, the essay-tales and the psychological studies are more characteristic of Hawthorne. Critics have in general conceded this fact, but have drawn from it far different deductions. It has been charged against Hawthorne that only rarely did he exert himself to put flesh and blood upon the skeleton of his ideas ; that for the most part he is a somewhat indolent dreamer, content to adumbrate his themes in listless essays and shadowy allegories. The charge of intellectual indolence, however, does not prove itself to the students of Hawthorne's notebooks, who there recognize with what elaborate patience he analyzed life and perfected his expression of it. The explanation of Hawthorne's aloofness must be sought elsewhere.

It can be found first of all in his Puritan inheritance, in that common temperament which made his mother also a recluse. He is the extreme example of the reflective Puritan, reinspired by Transcendentalism. He is peculiar only because he is extreme, and because he illustrates the type with so

B

little complexity. It should be remembered that Emerson and Thoreau, for all their inwardness of observation, were practical men ; but Hawthorne never lived in any other world than his thought. He was contemplative all the time, as the old Puritan was half the time. The Puritan, through aiming to accomplish the will of God, formed the habit of much conscientious self-scrutiny, in order to be sure that he knew what the will of God was. With the central doctrine of Transcendentalism, that nature in all its aspects exists not in itself outside of us, but in our apprehension of it, the Puritan's obligation to examine his own heart was reinforced. In Hawthorne, as in Emerson, the obligation was further strengthened by sympathy with the new scientific mood. Indeed New England Transcendentalism would be sorely misinterpreted if it were taken as a mere sport of the idealistic spirit, for much of its appeal came from its prophetic recognition of materialism. This belief, for example, that the true experience was within, not outside, the soul was bound up with the conception of the universe as so much fixed stimulus, reaching through various channels of touch to the inner consciousness that interprets it. This scientific attitude and the Transcendental mood and the old Puritan temper, all met in Hawthorne, and the combination mastered him. In his characteristic moments he was preoccupied with the effect of life upon himself, and he emphasized the need of solitude for such preoccupation. When he ventured into society or into the active world, it was by way of submitting his nature to some new stimulus, for the satisfaction of scientific curiosity. The effect of action was so much more important to him than action itself that he found his vocation only in meditating. A life so inward did not, however, entirely satisfy him; at times he was uncomfortably conscious of a difference between himself and other men, and craved some actual contact with life, some work with his hands, which would reassure him of his affinity with his fellows. But even manual toil became unreal to him as soon as habit had dulled its stimulus, and he longed to be free from the uninterpreted routine to pursue his isolated meditation. It is not surprising, then, nor is it to his discredit, that his characteristic stories set forth the minimum of incident with the maximum of significance. When he came, he even saves himself the delay necessary for reproducing the incident, and begins at once to interpret it. The result is hardly a story. But it is not really an essay, either. It is always an interpretation of one concrete experience, with the concrete experience tending to omit itself; it is never an abstraction of several incidents.

If Hawthorne temperamentally was averse to active life, at least one result of the publishing of *Twice Told Tales* was to furnish him with an excellent reason for being practical. The book drew the attention of the Peabodys, who had formerly been neighbours of the Hawthornes, but had lost sight of them during the year in Maine. Elizabeth Peabody, the remarkable elder daughter of the family, took steps to renew the acquaintance, and the two households became intimate. Mary Peabody, who later became the wife of the educator, Horace Mann, seems overshadowed in the family memory by Elizabeth's strong personality, but Sophia, the youngest sister, was somewhat set apart by invalidism and by delicacy of nature. All who recall her make her seem exquisite. When Hawthorne with his sisters first visited the Peabody home, Elizabeth tried to persuade Sophia to come downstairs and greet them, saying that the young writer was splendid-looking, handsomer than Byron. That evening Sophia could not see him, but he came again, and Elizabeth recorded the scene. " This time she came down, in her simple white wrapper, and sat on a sofa. As I said, ' My sister Sophia,' he rose and looked at her intently—he did not realize how intently. As we went on talking, she would frequently interpose a remark, in her low sweet voice. Every time she did so, he would look at her again, with the same piercing indrawing gaze. I was struck with it, and thought, ' What if he should fall in love with her ! ' And the thought troubled me ; for she had often told me that nothing would ever tempt her to marry and inflict on a husband the care of an invalid."

But Hawthorne soon persuaded Sophia Peabody to engage herself to him. The betrothal, however, was to be kept secret until he should make a more substantial place in the world. At this juncture his friends came to his aid, and got him the appointment as weigher and gauger in the Boston Custom House, where George Bancroft, the historian, was collector of the port. His duties began in January, 1839.

His diary gives the best account of this experience, which at first afforded him a pleasant though not enthusiastic sense of contact with actual life, and ended in complete dissatisfaction with the uninspiring routine. The minute accounts of the coal ships in which he did his weighing, and of the strong, individual men with whom he did his work, are at the beginning of his experience very important, as though he were recording phenomena for later meditation. But his suppressed personality soon reasserted itself. Within a year the diary becomes almost complaining. When his duties were changed from weighing coal to inspecting salt vessels, he wrote, " I am convinced that Christian's burden consisted of coal; and no wonder he felt relieved, when it fell off and rolled into the sepulchre." The chief significance, however, of Hawthorne's experience at the Boston Custom House as he recorded it in his journal is that he for a time strove to find his interest in the outer world. But in spite of his effort he gradually returned to his natural introspection.

In April, 1841, a change of administration ended his employment. The two years had not advanced his prospect of matrimony. In 1840 the Peabodys had moved to Boston, where Elizabeth Peabody started a bookshop and became the publisher of *The Dial*. Perhaps at her suggestion, Hawthorne had brought out, between November, 1840, and February, 1841, three books for children— *Grandfather's Chair*, *Famous Old People*, and *Liberty Tree*, a series of historical tales of early New England, written with an obvious educational purpose. During these two years he had accomplished no other writing, except the entries in his notebook. His only tangible profit was the sum of one thousand dollars (£200), which he had saved.

He immediately invested this sum in the Brook Farm colony, and joined the Transcendentalist experiment,—moved more by a properly selfish hope of finding a home to which to take a bride, than by great sympathy with the enterprise. His notebook, as usual, gives the inner history of his experience. He tried to learn farming, gladly did his share of the work, and enjoyed the society of the remarkable men and women gathered in the community. But within a month his life had become a burden. The leisure for writing which he had expected did not come, or was useless because he was so weary with bodily toil, and true to his temper, he craved opportunity to meditate and reflect. " Oh, labour is the curse of the world," he wrote, " and nobody can meddle with it without becoming proportionally brutified. Is it a praiseworthy matter that I have spent five golden months in providing food for cows and horses ? It is not so." In September he visited his people in Salem, already convinced that Brook Farm was doomed. When he returned to it, therefore, it was only to use it as a temporary lodging, and to do some unimportant writing. By the beginning of 1842, having no prospects except faith in his literary powers, and having lost the investment in Brook Farm, he and Sophia Peabody decided to share their poverty. They were married in Boston, July 9, 1842, and went at once to live at Concord, in the house called the Old Manse.

Here, where Emerson's grandfather had dwelt, and later Dr. Ezra Ripley, the Hawthornes led a very happy but very quiet life for three years. It is, perhaps, difficult to see how they met expenses, even by the austere frugality we know they practised. Just why Hawthorne wrote so little is at first hard to understand ; but doubtless his temperament needed leisure to meditate on the many new experiences that crowded his days. His journal shows how almost silenced his genius was in the happiness of his love. For neighbours he had Emerson and Margaret Fuller and the Ellery Channings ; some of his creative energy may have been drawn off in the brilliant talks with such stimulating friends. The old desire to toil with his hands he satisfied at last in a pleasant way, by helping his bride in household work or by caring for his garden. This was his daily life, practically, until 1843, when he resumed his writing. Besides editing his friend Bridge's *Journal of an African Cruiser*, he wrote many of the stories published in New York in 1846 under the title of *Mosses from an Old Manse*. It is not clear that all of these stories were written at this time, for the collection is different in no essential from *Twice Told Tales*. But before the appearance of this second collection Hawthorne was in actual need. His first child, Una, was born March 3, 1844; the increased expense of the family made it impossible to subsist mainly on the garden fruit and vegetables. At this juncture, one day in May, 1845, Horatio Bridge, who had been sponsor for the *Twice Told Tales*, came with Franklin Pierce to visit Hawthorne. They had had an idea that he must need help, and their visit by itself gave him cheerful encouragement. They found him working in his garden, and they insisted on romping with him, concealing the seriousness of their interest beneath a boylike manner of high spirits. The following summer Bridge used his political influence in his friend's behalf, and on March 23, 1846, Hawthorne was appointed Surveyor of the Salem Custom House.

In October, 1845, in expectation of the appointment, he had given up the Old Manse and returned to Salem, to share his home with his mother and sisters. As his family increased, he was forced to move into a separate, larger house, and then into a still larger one where his mother and sisters joined him. He and Sophia spent the late summer and autumn of 1846 in Boston, to be with the Peabodys, and during this visit the son, Julian, was born.

Hawthorne's new work allowed him more leisure than he had enjoyed at the Boston Custom House, and he entered upon his duties with more enthusiasm than usual, almost imagining, he said, that his Salem ancestors watched him, to see that he would prove himself a capable man. Until he was settled in his third and final house, he had no secluded place in which to write, and his literary work, therefore, for the first year amounted to nothing. But after November, 1847, he made a practice of writing something every day, and the immediate results were a number of short stories like those of the two earlier collections. The majority of these were published in Boston, 1852, under the title *The Snow Image and Other Twice Told Tales*. Besides this writing Hawthorne seems to have meditated much upon the theme of his first novel, but his duties at the Custom House daily prevented him from giving it the necessary continuous thought.

In June, 1849, with a change of political administration Hawthorne found himself out of office. Perhaps he would have been glad to be free, as he had been when relieved of his Boston post, but now his responsibilities were heavy, and, although he had managed to clear himself of all old debts, he had saved nothing. When he came home, however, and told his wife the discouraging news, she cheered him by her enthusiastic exclamation, "Oh, then you can write your book!" and showed him that without his knowledge she had saved a good sum from her household money. That afternoon he began *The Scarlet Letter.*

This romance is the most thoroughly thought out, the most completely mastered, of all Hawthorne's works. Yet it was composed in the least propitious circumstances. In July it was evident that his invalid mother was dying. Besides the mental distraction of his sorrow, Hawthorne had largely the care of the household, as his wife was busy nursing the invalid. Madame Hawthorne died the last day of July. Her illness had depleted the family purse; the romance was far from finished, and Hawthorne had no other assets. For the last time in his life he faced poverty. There is something unusually virile in the steadiness of nerve with which he worked at his book,—nine hours a day, as his wife tells us. But his predicament could not be concealed; and once more the friends whose faith in him had twice been his rescue gave him the opportunity to complete his work. George S. Hillard, who with his wife had been the first guests at the Old Manse, wrote to him January 17, 1850, enclosing a cheque which was, he said, to represent the debt Hawthorne's friends owed him for what he had done for American literature. This gift was probably the most humiliating kindness Hawthorne ever received, but he could not decline it, and in a manly letter to Hillard he accepted it as a loan. In December, 1853, he had the satisfaction of paying it back, with interest.

Four days after the receipt of Hillard's gift, *The Scarlet Letter* was finished. Before Hawthorne had taken it to a publisher, James T. Fields happened to call upon him, and asked for any available manuscript. After some hesitation Hawthorne produced the new book, which he had himself hardly read over. Field did not read very far before he accepted the great story, which he published in April, 1850.

Though not the most famous of American novels, *The Scarlet Letter* is by modern standards the greatest. It not only portrays a scene, but it contemplates a profound meaning in life. The theme is both subtle and striking, as very few of Hawthorne's themes are ; and it has an immense application beyond the place and time of the plot. Hawthorne's genius for meditation made in this novel an almost universal reach. Perhaps this universality might be found also in *The Marble Faun ;* but in the *The Scarlet Letter* the world is displayed with that conviction of reality which Hawthorne usually masters only in his dramatic short stories. Indeed, this story is considered by most critics as the ultimate example of the method illustrated in *The Gray Champion* and *Endicott and the Red Cross.*

The effect of life upon the soul was the central interest of all Hawthorne's speculations; and, as this effect is most formidable when the safety of the soul is most concerned, his characteristic theme became the study of sin. In no other story did he state the theme with quite so much power as in *The Scarlet Letter;* for Dimmesdale the clergyman, Hester Prynne the erring wife, and Chillingworth the wronged husband are all strongly developed characters, highly interesting even apart from this special crisis; and what each has done was done wilfully. The old physician wronged Hester when he compelled her to marry him—he himself tells us he wronged her; and that Hester and Dimmesdale knew their sin is equally clear. At first sight this plot would not seem to illustrate the power of life upon the passive soul; these souls are dramatically responsible for their actions. But Hawthorne is rarely interested in actions. In this novel he is fascinated not by the sins committed, but by their effect upon different people. Hester and Dimmesdale—to sum up the problem in brief space—shared the same sin, but Hester was punished for her guilt and Dimmesdale concealed his; what were the ultimate consequences for each?

Upon the original sin Hawthorne passes no judgment. The qualifying circumstances of the plot would have made it difficult for any moralist to render a verdict. Hester and Dimmesdale feel that their love had in it a consecration of its own. But the magic of Hawthorne's genius is in his ignoring of the actual sin, to contemplate which would have rendered the character of Hester less noble, and the fate of Dimmesdale less pathetic, and would have distracted attention from the real plot. Once the sin is committed and Chillingworth appears, Hester and Dimmesdale become victims of their sin; and Chillingworth, who in an indirect sense has caused the situation, becomes the malign personification of their past.

Criticism has analyzed the book in other terms, as a study of punishment. Hester suffers publicly for her fault, Dimmesdale secretly. Hester illustrates the inability of public vengeance to reach the sinner's heart. Dimmesdale shows the futility of private revenge, for by pursuing him Chillingworth saves him, and loses his own soul. The punishment that is effective comes from within and chastens with time; this seems to be the moral of the story. Dimmesdale at first is too cowardly to confess his guilt, but he stands on the scaffold at last and becomes a free man; Hester becomes almost a saint in patience and long suffering. From such points of view the book is hopeful. But to take these points of view one must forget the original sin, as Hawthorne forgot it; or the romance sets forth the difficult paradox of salvation through sin. This is not the only story in which Hawthorne suggests the problem of the good in evil.

The scarlet letter, the physical symbol about which plays so much fancy, had been described in *Endicott and the Red Cross,* where a young woman in the market place wears the shameful design on her bosom. The picturesque symbol had suggested the great romance. But the mood of Hawthorne's early work is revived chiefly in the contrasts between the past and the future, which largely give to *The Scarlet Letter* its thought-provoking quality. The Puritans were a radical people, as compared with Old England, but when once settled in their colony, they became conservative, even to the extent of persecuting all who disagreed with them. Against the Puritan background Hester and Dimmesdale, feeling after a modern theory of the individual's right to be happy, seem centuries younger than their young environment. The book is at heart radical, and what is great in it seems still to belong not to the old Puritan conscience, but to the future.

The success of this romance gave Hawthorne the position his genius deserved. Though not immediately enriched, he was relieved of financial worry, and could proceed with a free mind to his next story. At his mother's death he had determined to leave Salem for a more economical home. In the spring of 1850 he moved to a small house in Lenox, since burned down, where he lived for a year and a half, and where his youngest child, Rose, was born in the spring of 1851. His life was quiet. The friends whom he cared to see sought him out, but he made the most of his solitude. In August, 1850, he began his second novel, *The House of the Seven Gables*, and finished it January 26, 1851.

This novel he regarded as the most characteristic expression of his genius, because it is less gloomy than *The Scarlet Letter*, more complex and subtle. His readers have not agreed as to its being characteristic, but the book is undoubtedly subtle and in a pallid fashion cheerful. That is, there are gleams of wintry light in it, and the tragedy of the plot is, in a way, far off. It is essentially a study of age, as *The Scarlet Letter* was essentially a study of youth and of youth's radicalism. There is here none of that radical prophecy of the future out of the past, which the other work teaches us to look for. Youth does enter the story, in the persons of Holgrave and Phoebe and the child who buys gingerbread, but these are on the outskirts of the plot, which studies the effect of sin on succeeding generations, as *The Scarlet Letter* studied its immediate effects. The wrong that the first Pyncheon did to old Maule, and the curse that the dying Maule pronounced, reproduce themselves in each cycle of the Pyncheon family, sin and curse growing somewhat thinner and more phantasmal in each generation, until the day when Hepzibah opens her shop as a last help to her decayed fortunes.

The peculiarity of Hawthorne's treatment is that he portrays the sin in its ultimate consequences; as in the earlier novel, the causes that produce the sin, the characters of which it is the dramatic expression, are less to him than its influence upon the third and fourth generation. Not only does the effect of the curse persist, not only does God give the Pyncheons blood to drink, as Maule had promised, but the sin also reappears, from father to son, in a predisposition to evil. Whatever may be the outward cheerfulness of the story, Hawthorne imagined nothing more fatalistic than this recurring

F

affinity with evil in the Pyncheon family, after a hundred years.

The descendants of Maule, however, do not in every generation reappear as the victims. The tyranny of the Pyncheons directs itself against those of their own blood. In the section of their history which the novel displays, Clifford and Hepzibah suffer for their brother's wickedness ; and they feel it vain to flee from their destiny, because they carry with them both inheritances, the sin and the punishment. For this reason they are perpetually solitary figures, as indeed are all the characters in the story. Phoebe seems never really one with her lover ; nor do Hepzibah and Clifford seem to take up again their broken life ; nor does Uncle Venner, pleasant as he is, seem to have any real part with the household.

However dark the book is, its fascination was felt at once, and its popularity has endured next to that of *The Scarlet Letter*. Not nearly so much can be said of Hawthorne's third story, *The Blithedale Romance*, published in 1852. In this book, for once, he left his gloomy theme of the influence of sin ; and evidently his strength failed him when he stood on less tragic ground. The novel is a romantic version of his Brook Farm experiences, many of the incidents of which he transferred from his notebook.

The suicide episode is also from his notebook, from his Concord life, when the poet Ellery Channing, on the night of July 9, 1843, took him to help to search for the body of a girl who had drowned herself in the river near by. In the journal this incident is powerfully told ; and in the romance it is no less powerful, being, indeed, hardly changed at all. But the rest of the story is less effective than the journal accounts of Brook Farm, and apart from the fine character of Zenobia, the book is not greatly remembered.

In June, 1852, the Hawthornes returned to Concord, and took up their residence in the house known as The Wayside. The six months before had been spent in West Newton, near the scene of Brook Farm. Hawthorne now felt that he was settled permanently. The sad death of his sister Louisa, in a steamboat disaster on the Hudson, disposed him still further toward a retired life. In 1853, however, he was appointed Consul at Liverpool by his old friend, then President Pierce, and he took up his residence there in July.

His foreign notebooks record both his official life until August 31, 1857, and the two years of travel that followed the termination of his appointment. Those two years were spent chiefly in Italy, and furnished him with the knowledge of art and land-

scape which he used in his last book. He
stayed for a while in England, on the way
home, to complete the novel, and returned
to Concord in June, 1860, his story having
been published that spring.

The Marble Faun is not Hawthorne's
greatest romance; but it is generally considered most characteristic of him. It lacks
the grip on outer life which distinguishes
The Scarlet Letter, but it shows in an almost
exaggerated form Hawthorne's power to
trace the inward world, especially of a soul
that has sinned. What crime Miriam committed before the novel begins, we do not
know, nor what becomes of her afterward.
What Donatello's youth was like, his charming
family legend does not really tell us, nor
do we know what ultimately becomes of
him. But we do see with terrible vividness
how Miriam's past leads Donatello to murder,
and how his impulsive crime changes his
soul.

Donatello is the central person of the story,
not because of any dramatic capacity to
act, but because he is passive, illustrating
the power of experience upon its victim. He
suggests also a dark moral quandary; undoubtedly his crime and its consequences
developed in him a soul. This perplexing
accomplishment of good out of evil had been
illustrated in *The Scarlet Letter*, and had been

suggested in Hawthorne's lesser writings; it was a fitting theme for the last work of one who all his life had brooded, more than most Puritans, on the intricate relations of good and evil.

The story has a kind of surface richness in its constant reference to Rome and its art treasures; many a traveller has used the romance as a sort of guidebook. Hawthorne's appreciation of art, however, was amateurish; and the value of the book lies chiefly in his keen observation, not of works of art, but of their effect upon himself. The true richness of the novel is in the multiplicity of directions in which the influence of Donatello's crime is traced. The chain of circumstances that lead the most innocent member of the group to disclose her knowledge of the murder, and though a Protestant, to find peace of mind in the Roman confessional, are as true as they are paradoxical, and they illustrate most typically the mode of Hawthorne's thought.

This was his last novel. He did begin a new story, *The Dolliver Romance*, but he made little progress with it. He felt an eerie premonition that his life was over, and he could put little heart in his writing. When his family noticed that his faculties seemed to fail, they urged him to travel for recreation, and he started South with his friend and publisher, D. W. Ticknor. At Philadelphia, however, Ticknor suddenly died, and Hawthorne returned to Concord broken by the shock. In May, 1864, he was persuaded to travel to New Hampshire with his friend ex-President Pierce. On the 18th of the month they reached Plymouth, and stopped for the night. Early next morning Hawthorne was found dead in his bed.

He was buried at Concord, in Sleepy Hollow, on the 24th. Longfellow, Emerson, Lowell, and Holmes stood by his grave.

CHAPTER V

EDGAR ALLAN POE

EDGAR ALLAN POE has had the fortune, good
or bad, to be one of the storm-centres of
American criticism. Judgments upon his life
as well as upon his work have been excessive
in blame or defence. Even in the single camp
of his enemies or his friends, there are two
factions, who allow either their opinion of his
life to prescribe their approach to his writings, or the quality of his imagination to
colour their view of his life. In Europe, by
contrast, there has been but one literary
opinion of Poe. Criticism there, without
exaggerating his range, has generously insisted
upon his rare mood and his finished art ;
indeed, to the French or Russian reader he is
usually the one American poet of significance.
And at last the persuasion grows upon even
the most prejudiced of his countrymen that,
if the American temper to some extent has
rejected Poe and the temper of Europe to a
large extent has welcomed him, the proper
inference, whatever it may be, is not neces-

sarily to Poe's discredit. The obligation upon the critic is clear—to understand Poe as he is envisaged abroad, and to explain that in him and in his countrymen which has qualified his fame at home.

They must excel in the disposition to judge their brother who would dare estimate Poe's exact accountability for the mismanagement of his life. He was born in Boston, January 19, 1809. The fact that his parents were actor folk, playing unsuccessfully in the city at the time, predestined him to no cordial acceptance by New England. That his father, David Poe, had been cast off by his very reputable family in Baltimore when he went on the stage would be no recommendation to Southern society. The mother, Elizabeth Arnold, was herself the daughter of an actress, and in 1805, when David Poe married her, she was the widow of another actor named Hopkins. All these theatrical people were unsuccessful, and David Poe married in desperate romantic improvidence. After a few years of hardship he died, or at least disappeared ; and at the end of 1811, while acting in Richmond, Mrs. Poe died, and Edgar was taken as a charity waif into the home of Mr. John Allan, a fairly well-to-do Scotch tobacco merchant, whose name he added to his own.

That he was a spoiled child in this family,

encouraged to exhibit his accomplishments of declamation and of drinking the health of guests ; that he spent five years in an English school, where he learned the use of his fists, and accumulated impressions of Old-World architecture and atmosphere ; that he was sent to the University of Virginia, where the social barrier between him and the well-born Southern boys fixed in his nature that obsession of morbid and sensitive pride which he makes almost a cardinal virtue in his stories, —these, with his inheritance of waywardness, are perhaps the controlling facts in his life. When in 1826, because of his drinking and gambling, Mr. Allan took him out of the University, Poe's character was already shaped. The Scotchman had never understood his protégé, as he proved by making the youth a clerk in his business. Poe immediately ran away.

After a short stay in Boston, where he published his first volume, *Tamerlane and Other Poems*, 1827, Poe enlisted in the army under the name of Edgar A. Perry. In his new way of life he succeeded better than might have been expected, and even earned promotion; but in 1829 he was sufficiently reconciled to Mr. Allan to profit by his influence in obtaining an honourable discharge, whereupon he applied for an appointment to West Point, meanwhile publishing his second volume, *Al*

Aaraaf, Tamerlane, and Minor Poems, Baltimore, 1829. From July, 1830, to February, 1831, he was at the military academy, disliking his duties more and more. He procured his dismissal by deliberate insubordination, and began his lifework in literature, with the New York edition of his *Poems*, 1831.

It was in Baltimore and with his prizestory, however—*The MS. Found in a Bottle*—that Poe's fame began, although circumstances brought it about that his reputation should for a time grow chiefly from editing and reviewing, rather than from verse or fiction. After a few contributions to the *Baltimore Saturday Visitor*, the magazine whose prize he had won, he became editor of the *Southern Literary Messenger*, which through his guidance, and especially after his notable review of a novel by one of the Knickerbocker school, in 1835, became the acknowledged rival of the best Northern magazines. His connection with this Richmond periodical coincided with the happiest period of his life. He is thought to have married privately, in 1835, his cousin Virginia Clemm, whose mother, his father's sister, had for some time shared his fortunes, and as long as he lived was his most helpful friend. He certainly married his cousin publicly in May, 1836, and his home life was ideal. His advancement in his profession seemed sure. He was

reckoned with as the founder of a new school
of severe and methodical criticism, and he was
demonstrating his unusual editorial gift for
developing a magazine.   But in the beginning
of 1837 his position on the *Messenger* was
abruptly   vacated,   in   consequence   of   a
drunken fit that incapacitated him for several
days.   After a brief but unhappy interval, he
became editor of *The Gentleman's Magazine*,
of Philadelphia, and demonstrated again his
skill in building up the periodical ; but again
he retired abruptly after a quarrel with the
owner of the magazine, the cause of which is
not known but easily guessed at.   He certainly had opportunities to recover himself
if self-control had been possible for him.   After
another interval he began to edit the new
Graham's Magazine, in which he published,
among other things, *The Murders in the Rue
Morgue*, and *The Descent into the Maelstrom*.
His chief service to the magazine, however,
was editorial, and he had his usual success ;
the subscriptions increased and his reputation spread.   But in 1842 he drank himself
out of this position also.   He had an excuse
for his weakness now ; his young wife had
broken a blood-vessel and had sunk into that
desperate invalidism from which she was
never to recover.   It was in his insanity over
the prospect of her death, Poe claimed, that he
turned to drink.   " My enemies," he said,

" referred the insanity to the drink, rather than the drink to the insanity."

The incident practically closed his opportunities in Philadelphia, though he enlisted the support of some patient friends in a scheme for a new magazine, and he encouraged himself in the hope that he might get a sinecure position with the Government. He also began a correspondence with Lowell, to whose short-lived magazine, *The Pioneer*, he contributed. But, on a visit to Washington, Poe disposed of his chances with the Government by getting drunk, and the failure of *The Pioneer*, perhaps, helped to discourage his publishing scheme. He made a brief adventure in lecturing, which was successful except financially, and he published his well-known *Black Cat* in *The Saturday Evening Post*, then called *The United States Saturday Post*. But he could not support himself by such meagre performance, and in what seems a desperate mood he settled in New York, in April, 1844.

His arrival was signalized by the publication of *The Balloon Hoax* in *The Sun*, April 13. For a time, he secured no permanent employment. In October, N. P. Willis gave him a very minor post on *The Evening Mirror*, a daily with a weekly supplement. In this paper on January 29, 1845, appeared *The Raven*, in comparison with the immediate

and permanent fame of which his previous
reputation is insignificant. Willis recognized
Poe's genius and remained his friend, but the
work of a daily paper was distasteful, and
Poe soon went over to *The Broadway Journal,*
a weekly managed by Charles F. Briggs, a
friend of Lowell's. Poe's connection with this
periodical is chiefly remembered for his
fanatical attacks upon Longfellow, whom
for years he had persistently accused of pla-
giarism. This unwarranted animosity was a
heavy charge upon the patience of his well-
wishers; and when Lowell, passing through
the city, called upon him and found him too
intoxicated to be seen, the inevitable end of
his career was fairly plain to all reasonably
skilful prophets. *The Broadway Journal* suddenly stopped, because Poe indulged in a
drunken spree, according to Briggs, and
Briggs was unwilling to go on with him. The
printer resumed publication, however, with
Poe as editor; and in October Poe bought the
rights of the Journal from the printer for
fifty dollars, and for one short space of his life
attained his ambition to own a periodical.
But he had absolutely no capital; in fact,
he had made his purchase with a promissory
note endorsed by Horace Greeley, who later
had to pay it; and after borrowing desper-
ately from a few friends open to his appeal,
Poe had to abandon his journal at the end of

the year. In October also, on the 16th, he had made his notorious appearance at the Boston Lyceum, where he had mystified an originally well-disposed audience by reading to them his *Al Aaraaf ;* and in *The Broadway Journal* for November 1 he followed up this strange performance by asserting that he had passed off a juvenile production upon the Boston people because they deserved nothing better. Altogether the year was most disastrous, although it closed with the publication of *The Raven and Other Poems* in New York.

In the beginning of 1846, Poe removed to the cottage at Fordham now visited as the chief shrine of his memory. There his wife's long illness soon became very serious, he himself approached a condition of collapse, and his poverty was extreme. His friends made a public appeal on his behalf, which wounded his pride, but he was in no position to refuse their charity. On January 30, 1847, his wife died. The remainder of his life is almost too pitiable to recount. What writing he did, even his philosophical *Eureka, A Prose Poem,* 1848, and the oft-declaimed poem, *The Bells,* is negligible. That his body and mind were shattered is the clear excuse for the maudlin love-making that occupied his last days. He wavered between an old flame of his Richmond youth and Mrs. Sarah Helen Whitman, of Providence, and in the end he

seems to have engaged himself in succession
to both.   They, as well as his other friends,
apparently tried to encourage him and rescue
his genius from himself ; but his long sufferings and his excesses brought him to a sudden
death in the Baltimore City Hospital, October 7, 1849.

A career so unedifying needs to be outlined
here only to explain Poe's reputation and,
perhaps, his work.   His character fared very
badly at the hands of Griswold, his first and
most ungenerous biographer ; and a life like
his easily attracts to itself mythical but no
less damaging accretions.   Yet even with
proper allowance Poe was handicapped with
American readers, who naturally made their
approach to his writings through the preju-
dicing vestibule of his personal reputation.
It would be out of place here to raise the
question whether the American insistence
upon a clean life in literary men is provincial, if not parochial, or whether it involves a
confusion of the values of art ; it is enough to
recognize that this insistence has distinguished
American literature and shaped its reputations.   Against the difference between his
character and that of Hawthorne, it has
availed Poe nothing that his stories are in
subject more conventional, and raise less moral
questioning, than Hawthorne's ; even were
his drunkenness and fondness for literary

imposture all a myth, it would still be remembered that he tried to injure Longfellow
and deceived Lowell. It may be that future
disclosures will render him on the personal
side a less discreditable figure.

Foreign readers, by contrast, have allowed
Poe's stories and poems to plead for themselves, and have attended to his life as a
secondary matter. This attitude seems at
once more just and kind, and it gives most
illumination. It permits us to see in all of
his best work an intellectual grip on the
details of expression—what is called technique
—and on the direction of the theme as a whole
—what is called form—such as no other
Anglo-Saxon writer has so habitually displayed. If his conscious art seems less
remarkable now, when the short story and the
short poem at the hand of an army of devotees
have been polished and finished to a point
of exhausted interest, it must be remembered that in such matters Poe largely showed
the way, and even prophesied that his methods
faithfully pursued, would lead to this widespread mastery of his craft. It is the
craftsman that we see in him first ; it is the
craftsman's creed that he formulates in the
Philosophy of Composition—a creed no less
valid because the particular account of
the composition of *The Raven* may not be
true. It should be added, for greater light on

his fame, that craftsmanship is the part of literature most easily taught and by the mediocre most readily apprehended.

This very appeal to the sense of technique has undoubtedly deprived Poe of some just recognition in America where the faith in the immediate inspiration of art has been somewhat exclusively held. Foreign readers, however, have observed that intellect in his work counts for far more than technique. The very subject-matter of his stories, for example, and the very mood that prompts them, are in essence intellectual. To say that his first writings suggest an imaginative flight in mathematics would be apt analogy, provided that the reader sees in mathematics something more than arithmetic. The mathematician steadily contemplates an eternity of order, to which temporal happenings are to be referred. To the mind that can perceive the eternal order all motley processions of events and haphazard multitudes of phenomena yield up the secret of their design, and can be rearranged to illustrate it. The delight of discovering in the apparently accidental world about us the analogue of the eternal order in our minds is the greatest—and in some form or other the commonest—of human lures. It is the motive alike of the scientist reconstructing Behemoth from a fossil tooth, and of the child solving a jig-saw puzzle. To perceive in life what the mind recognizes as order is, of course, the function of literature as well as of mathematics. But the poet loves human phenomena as well as the truth to be seen through them; his affection tries to make them eternal, as well as the truth; whereas the mathematician gladly exchanges life for symbols, if thereby he can more clearly demonstrate what life has taught him. In practically all his stories Poe, like a mathematician, makes a demonstration, and in order to prove his theorem with the absoluteness that mathematics rather than literature requires, he deals not with characters but with symbols.

The illustrations are easy to find. Few of the tales have their suggestion from observation—what is ordinarily called experience; they usually start from speculation induced by reading, and the speculation or the passage that suggested it is, at the beginning, like a proposition to be proved. *Morella*, the study of persistent identity, has a motto from Plato, " Itself, by itself, one everlastingly, and single "; and the tale shows us how a dying mother, by abnormal exercise of the will, took possession of the new-born daughter, so that they were identical. *Ligeia*, the best example, starting from a saying of Joseph Glanville's, that " Man doth not yield himself to the angels, nor unto death utterly, save only through the weakness of his feeble will," demonstrates how the soul of a passionate woman long dead returned to her husband's side by appropriating the dying body of his second wife, even changing it back to her own appearance. There is no need to point out that the characters in these stories are symbols, or that the events are shaped to effect a kind of proof. Even in the tales that seem different, there is no other method. In *The Masque of the Red Death*, where the design to be elucidated is one of colour, the theme to be proved is stated in the early description of the pestilence : " Blood was its avatar and its seal—the redness and the horror of blood." In *The Cask of Amontillado*, which demonstrates a theory of revenge, the theory is first advanced : " A wrong is unredressed when retribution overtakes its redresser. It is equally unredressed when the avenger fails to make himself felt as such to him who has done wrong." No less clear is the method of imagination-demonstration in the pseudo-scientific tales, like *The MS. Found in a Bottle*, or *The Descent into the Maelstrom*, or *Hans Pfall ;* and the method is even more palpable in the tales of ratiocination, such as *The Murders in the Rue Morgue.*

Poe was conscious of the kinship of his art to mathematics, and he well knew that it would produce a powerful effect of inevitability. He tells us in *The Philosophy of Composition* how he wrote : " I prefer commencing with the consideration of an *effect*. . . . Having chosen a novel, first, and secondly a vivid effect, I consider whether it can be best wrought by incident or tone—whether by ordinary incidents and peculiar tone, or the converse, or by peculiarity both of incident and tone—afterward looking about me (or rather within) for such combinations of event, or tone, as shall best aid me in the construction of the effect." And later, speaking of *The Raven*, he says, " It is my design to render it manifest that no one point in its composition is referable either to accident or intuition ; that the work proceeded, step by step, to its completion with the precision and rigid consequence of a mathematical problem." Where every step proceeds with this precision and consequence, a story must have that inevitability which is the secret of literary form—that fatedness which has chiefly fascinated the genius of Greece and of France— nations that, significantly, have been devoted also to mathematics. In Poe this inevitability of form, perhaps, encouraged a preference for subjects in which fate could be exploited ; and in his themes of doom he appeals to the French, as he would have appealed to the Greeks.

The obvious criticism of all this method is
that Poe has little interest in life as it is, and
remains aloof from common human affairs.
He chiefly looked within himself, as he has
just told us, for his facts. With few excep-
tions his stories do not proceed through conversation, nor through any other exhibition
of reality; his business was not to see the
real, but to make us see the fanciful as if it
were real, in order to prove his point. His
persons are phantom symbols; he does not
know them, nor do we; who is Usher, apart
from his disease? or Dupin, apart from his
skill? Yet these objections to Poe's method
are best made when we have not recently read
him. The fact is, if each story begins by ap-
pealing to the mind, it ends by taking hold of
the soul. In the process of reading we cannot
escape a profound *emotional* experience—
that effect which Poe said was his first intention. When we analyse them, the elements
of his skill are rigid and cold as the type on
the page; the story, however, is not on the
page but in us. In other words, it is a mistake not to distinguish between the intellectual process of the demonstration and the
emotional effect of it. Intellectually *The
Murders in the Rue Morgue* exploits the ratio-
cinative method; as a work of art it takes
hold of us with the horror of the incident and
the scene. Intellectually *The Descent into the*

Maelstrom expounds the principles of physics which saved the fisherman from the whirlpool ; the effect of the story is the profound terror of the predicament. To say, therefore, that Poe's art remains aloof from experience is to forget that it always lays its finger on some sensitive nerve of the reader's spirit.

Moreover, Poe does give us a remarkable disclosure of life in the revelation of his own nature. Perhaps it would be better for his fame, though hardly for his morbid charm, if this were not so. All his great stories exhibit some triumph or attitude of the mind, yet their effect is one of horror. That his psychological interest and the practice of his own intellect led Poe to the creation of horror is the chief index of something fearsome, something demon-like in him. To that age and that land that has habitually dreamt of the beneficence of science, Poe was the prophet of science as a Frankenstein, and of all horizons of the mind as so many possible avenues to hell. Little wonder that his countrymen found in this function of his genius something malign ; less wonder, perhaps, that they have held to their first opinion, seeing what manner of person he draws to him from abroad, beginning with his French sponsor, Baudelaire. Of the moral conventions of his times Poe was never a foe, and his writings are, in a quiescent way, the very

strongholds of propriety; unlike the New
England Puritans, he is so sure of the validity
of the Ten Commandments that he always
assumes it without discussion. But in a
deeper sense he shakes our faith in life; crime
he discovers on every hand, but ignores its
moral aspects as sin; worst of all, he is sus-
picious of life, of the mind itself, as of something that may at any moment betray the
soul.

The other less fundamental ways in which
Poe has written his own portrait can only be
enumerated here. So often his theme is the
power of the will to surmount obstacles that
even the least subtle reader is aware of Poe's
brooding on his own weakness, and of the ideal
strength he set before himself. His hero, too,
like himself, seems dedicated to some strange
fate, and is a solitary spirit. He is almost
as prophetic of his doom as Shelley was.
He often reverts to the lover who after his
bride's death forgets her and marries again;
whether the outcome is happy, as in *Eleonora,*
or weird, as in *Ligeia,* there is a troubled emphasis upon the sin of disloyalty. More
obvious studies of his worse self are found in
William Wilson and *The Imp of the Perverse.*
Criticism has also stressed the autobiography
in the low physical tone to which so many of
the stories are keyed—the atmosphere of disease and invalidism and epileptic seizure,—

and for a brighter record, the tenacious worship of an ideal beauty even in the most pathetic discouragements.

Poe's critical principles have been implied in what has here been said of his stories, for his theory is for the most part a very subtle analysis of his own practice. The end of poetry, he taught, is to express the yearning for the beautiful—the desire not of the beauty we see, but of the beauty we dream. Therefore poetry—and he meant the term to include all great art—is necessarily freed from any obligation to fact ; the poet may change the occurrences of life as he pleases, in order to reproduce the ideal. " We struggle by multiform combinations among the things and thoughts of Time to attain a portion of that Loveliness whose very elements, perhaps, appertain to Eternity alone." The purpose of this combination and rearrangement is to show " a harmony where none was apparent before," to make that demonstration of the eternal order which we noticed in the stories. The function of the intellect, as far as poetry is concerned, is to manage this demonstration ; the resulting effect of the whole, however, is emotional. The eternal order may also be conceived as truth or goodness, but not primarily so in poetry ; the poet, having pursued the eternal order with passionate emotion, sees it not as truth but as

beauty.   Therefore—and this still is to many
Anglo-Saxons a stumbling-block—beauty is
more to the poet than morals or duty or conscience or truth; beauty includes these
others, but it alone should be the immediate
goal.   Even truth, for the poet, is valuable
chiefly as a means of approach to the eternal
order; the order itself is beauty.   Poe sums
up his theory in one sentence: " And in
regard to Truth—if, to be sure, through the
attainment of a truth we are led to perceive a
harmony where none was apparent before, we
experience at once the true poetical effect;
but this effect is referable to the harmony
alone, and not in the least degree to the truth
which merely served to render the harmony
manifest."   And the poet differs from the
prose artist only in that his province is the
rhythmical creation of beauty.

In stating this theory Poe developed a
secondary theory, which has usually had
a larger share of attention.   The effect of a
poem is to excite, by elevating the soul.   All
excitement is, of necessity, transient.   When
the excitement dies, the elevation of soul
ends—and so does the poem, in so far as it
is a poem.   Therefore a long poem does not
exist; the epics are simply a collection of
different excitements, different poems.   On
the other hand, some poems are too short,
because they end before the excitement has

run its course. The perfect poem has an absolute unity of form, in that it conveys a single excitement as the excitement occurs, without expansion or compression.

The essay or lecture, *The Poetic Principle*, in which his theory is set forth, marks the serious beginning of literary criticism in the United States. It remains the most important of American contributions to critical theory. Though its ideas are familiar enough now to the professed student of literature, they are still at variance with the common practice of American poets, and of all but the best English poets; and some readers still resent that Poe should find fault with Longfellow for didacticism. In another essay, *The Philosophy of Composition*, he advances the not very startling paradox that all stories and poems must be written backwards. The main interest of the essay lies in the brilliant account of the writing of *The Raven*. Probably few people believe that the process was as Poe tells us; perhaps he had convinced himself that it was. But if the account may not be true of the method of the poem, it is a remarkable analysis of the poem's effect.

A third essay, on *The Rationale of Verse*, makes some pedantic display of Poe's ideas of metre, and also shows an admirable grasp of the difference between classical quantitative verse and English stress verse. These

three essays constitute Poe's achievement in
critical theory, and his just fame as a critic
largely rests on them. But his immediate
reputation rested on his particular criticisms,
—on his reviews of Longfellow and Hawthorne and lesser Americans, on his clever
prophecy of the plot of *Barnaby Rudge*, and
his later analysis of the book, and on his early
recognition of Tennyson and Mrs. Browning
and others not then arrived at fame. Even in
his least pleasant reviews, where his irritability
and almost insane prejudices make the reading unbearably bitter, his acuteness of observation is extraordinary. As in the case of
his master Coleridge, his literary intuitions
are always fine, whatever may be thought of
the reasoning by which he supports them.

One criticism of Poe's poetic practice is
suggested by his poetic theory. The worth
of any poem must depend, not upon the
truth incidentally treated—for by definition
Poe is not concerned with the incidental
truth—but upon the total effect of truth,
which is beauty. Safe as this formula is for
the analysis of a poem of which the effect
is unquestioned, it contains no certain recipe
for getting the effect. The most didactic
rhymster has this advantage over Poe, that he
can be understood even by the imaginative
who despise him, whereas Poe, if his reader
through lack of sympathy or imagination

misses the effect, often seems to say nothing at all. Hence there are two very different attitudes toward his poetry, and most of his readers by change of mood have gone over from one side to the other.

A few poems, however, have been so sure and so permanent in their effect that Poe is not likely to rank second to any other American poet, even the most voluminous. An improvement of literary taste in the reader may, indeed, make Poe's domain seem narrower; but it will also establish him more firmly in his range, and the poems that miss their effect will be fewer. Those that seem now most secure of their fame are *Israfel* and the shorter poem *To Helen*. The effect, rather than the idea, of both is that poignant yearning after the ideal which is the essence of poetry. Poe wrote nothing more ethereal, more vibrant, more inevitable in form than *Israfel*; it is also the most manly in tone of all his poems, and is often considered the finest. *To Helen*, known by its two much-quoted lines, is more artificial, less soaring, and less confiding of his character. A little below these two, because of a certain unevenness, are *To One in Paradise*, with its splendid cadence, and *The Haunted Palace* memorable for the eerie music of its second stanza.

Eulalie, Ulalume, and *Annabel Lee* have

been much associated with *The Bells* as subjects of parody ; but they differ from the well-known sound-poem in being far more than an opportunity for the elocutionist. They express that passionate sorrow for a dead woman which was a prophetic theme in all Poe's work. This strange obsession has been referred to the premature death in his boyhood of a woman who had befriended him. At all events, Poe's mind strangely occupied itself from his youth—as Rossetti's did—with this state of bereavement which he later signally realized.

In this theme, indeed, the lives of Rosetti and Poe cross, for *The Blessed Damozel*, as Hall Caine tells us, was suggested by *The Raven*. Rossetti saw that Poe had done the utmost with the grief of the lover on earth, and determined to reverse the situation and describe the grief of the lover in heaven. To some readers this fortunate suggestion will seem the chief merit of *The Raven ;* to the imaginative and sympathetic, Poe's best known poem will seem what it really is, one of the most original of human records of despair.

CHAPTER VI

THE TRANSCENDENTALISTS

THE Transcendentalist movement in New
England must be studied as an attitude in
individuals, rather than as a philosophical
creed. Hardly any two Transcendentalists
believed exactly the same doctrines, or
brought their arguments from the same
source. The movement seems to have been
a natural emancipation from a worn-out
theology; Puritanism in Massachusetts had
run its course; that the religious genius of
the serious community should seek a new
development, was natural enough.

The ease with which the change arrived
indicates, probably, that its significance was
not realized. Some devout persons shared
the new ideas without feeling any need to
abandon their old theological ground; such
a person in particular was the great Dr.
William Ellery Channing (1780-1842), whose
pulpit had a wider influence in New England
than Emerson's lecture platform. Almost
all the Transcendentalists took with them,

even when they left their old religion, the mood of that religion, without any apparent thought of incongruity. This quietness of manner excites some admiration. Emerson and his congregation, when they parted, showed a fine moral poise, a Christian good-will in their irreconcilable differences. But the incongruity between the old mood and the new ideas of Transcendentalism suggests also at times a somewhat amusing immaturity; and people with a strong sense of humour do not always find it easy to take Emerson or Margaret Fuller or Alcott as seriously as they deserve. The weakness of the Transcendentalists in this respect is more apparent when they are brought into contrast with European characters, whose vision was naturally broader. Carlyle's comments upon his Transcendentalist visitors seem to prick some false bubble—though just what bubble, it is not at first easy to see.

The truth is that Transcendentalism in New England was a parochial manifestation. It made its way in communities so much less than provincial that they still thought in terms of the parish, and even insisted on the dignity of the parish in human thought. It is, no doubt, true that human nature in Concord would be much like human nature in Athens; yet there is a differ ence between the Transcendentalist attitude which vigorously asserted the equality of Concord, and the equanimity of Socrates which assumed Athens without discussion. The Athenian, living in the best world he knew, did not think to defend it ; the Transcendentalist, realizing larger and older civilizations beyond the village borders, yet set up the village by way of challenge to the world. To recognize this at the outset need not diminish any true admiration for Emerson's greatness or Thoreau's ; and the admission will perhaps prepare for an explanation of the Transcendental incongruities of religion and philosophy.

The chief of the Transcendentalists was Ralph Waldo Emerson, born in Boston, May 25, 1803. His father, William Emerson, was a distinguished clergyman in the city, as his grandfather also had been in Concord. By all the family traditions he was dedicated to the pulpit from his birth. At his father's early death, the care of the family fell upon the mother and Miss Mary Emerson, that famous aunt of whom later Emerson wrote lovingly. Some encouragement came also from Dr. Ezra Ripley, minister of Concord, who had married the widow of the grandfather Emerson. But for the most part the children had to know poverty, even to the extent of suffering jeers from other boys for their lack of proper clothing. Their aunt Mary, however, turned the poverty to good account in their moral education, and they early learned a Spartan superiority over circumstances.

William Emerson, the eldest son, was graduated from Harvard in 1818, and started a young ladies' school in Boston in order to pay for the education of Ralph Waldo, who had entered Harvard in 1817. The younger brother helped in his own support by various work in college ; and when the menial nature of his service—waiting on table, for example—humiliated him, Miss Mary Emerson preached to him a truer kind of pride. Doubtless this discipline was a large part of his benefit from college, for he was not a distinguished scholar. When he left Cambridge he took charge for a while of his brother's school, in order to permit William to continue his studies for the ministry. This pedagogical experience taught Ralph how awkward he was, how out of sympathy with the conventional society represented by his girl pupils. He was glad to close the school in 1825, and begin his residence as a divinity student at Cambridge. He had worn himself out, however, with too confined application, and he was obliged to spend some time on a farm, to recover his health. Then he did some teaching for a while to lay up money for further

H

study; and in the beginning of 1826 he took the place of his brother Edward, who had been conducting a school at Roxbury, and who at this time also broke down. With all these distractions Emerson saw but little of the Divinity School; but his general reading and his high character seem to have satisfied the authorities, and in October, 1826, he was " approbated to preach " by the Middlesex Association of Ministers. Because his eyes were very weak, he was excused from examination.

For a time there seemed little chance that he could undertake active work. So desperate was his physical condition that he was sent south for the winter, and when he returned the following spring he was unable to do more than occasional preaching. Meanwhile several events in the family added to his personal discouragements. His older brother, William, intended for the ministry, had outgrown his orthodox faith, as Emerson was later destined to do, and had disappointed the family by turning to the law. Although Edward's health had been regained, it was likely at any moment to be lost again, so ambitious was he in his studies. In 1828 he went insane; and though he recovered his reason, his prospects were ruined. Of these spiritual and physical upsets, Emerson realized that he as well as his brothers might be in danger, but something of his bright philosophy already aided him; he managed to make headway against ill health, and even had the courage to engage himself, in December, 1828, to Miss Ellen Louise Tucker, herself an invalid. In the following March he was ordained associate pastor with the Rev. Henry Ware, of the Old North Church in Boston, and on September 30 he was married. Dr. Ware shortly afterward left him in sole charge of the parish. He was made chaplain of the Massachusetts Senate, as his father had been. In outward things he had suddenly entered upon bright prospects.

During the three years that Emerson held his pastorate his character was developed and fixed in its final moulds. It would seem to be in keeping with the sunniness of his disposition and his philosophy that this development came not from the discipline of adversity, but from his own conscience. Some lucky fate had allowed him to go thus far in his ministerial life without a single challenge; he had even escaped the ordinary examinations when he was allowed to preach. But now that the care of souls was fully upon him, he began to question his own position. It is significant of the gradual break-up of orthodoxy in New England that his congregation patiently suffered his more and more

radical sermons, and the younger people
even delighted in them, although some of
the older folk began to feel uneasy. At
last he decided to lay his scruples frankly
before his congregation ; and in June, 1832,
he proposed that the church thereafter celebrate the sacrament without the elements.
His congregation did not agree to the plan,
and he felt bound to resign. Between him
and his associate, Dr. Ware, and all of the
parish, there continued to be friendship and
good-feeling, and the congregation were sorry
that he should leave them. Once later he
almost undertook regular parish work, but the
engagement became impossible when he
stipulated that he should say prayers in the
church only when he was in the mood.

His sorrow at leaving his church, almost
his profession, was lost at the time in his
greater grief for his wife, who had died on
February 8, 1831. To recover himself he
made his first trip abroad, and saw Landor,
Coleridge, Wordsworth, and above all, Carlyle, whom he visited at Craigenputtock.
On his return to Boston in October, 1833,
he lived with his mother, preached occasional
sermons, and supported himself by lecturing.
From 1834 to 1835 he and his mother lived
with Dr. Ezra Ripley at the Old Manse,
his grandfather Emerson's house, which Hawthorne later occupied. On September 14,

1835, he married Miss Lydia Jackson, of Plymouth, and removed to the home he had bought for himself in Concord. With his new start in life came new sorrows, in the deaths of his brilliant younger brothers,— Edward dying in Porto Rico, and Charles, of quick consumption, in New York. Though he was living in his boyhood scenes, Emerson had been cut loose from his past, and was ready to appear in a new character.

In 1836 he published his first book, *Nature*, upon which he had for some years been writing. In this little volume, half essay in spirit, half poem, can be found the germs of his later thinking, and even in his solider work he never again made so imaginative an appeal. He writes of the uses of nature, considering the universe as commodity of beauty or language; but his real theme is the independence and unity of man. It is our habit, he says, to look too much to the past. Our humble desire to learn leads to an unprofitable retrospection, to mere building sepulchres of the fathers. The past cannot aid us, because we inherit its error as well as its progress. The answer to our problems lies rather in our present selves. " Everyman's condition is a solution in hieroglyphics to those inquiries he would put." This faith in the total equipment of the individual is the basis of Emerson's doctrine of the Over-Soul, the divine in man.

To be free of the past, however, Emerson found that man must go into solitude, for society is the authentic representative of the past. Solitude, or that kind of society which is most like solitude, is the condition of the soul's freedom to question and answer itself. To Emerson society was full of what Carlyle called " old clothes ; " but the American would hardly allow that there was anything else in it, whereas Carlyle would reform it, he would leave it. Nor would Emerson fear lest nature, apart from society, should be inadequate to man's wants ; nature is the greatest of commodities, and her bounty is a perpetual rebuke to that mismanagement by which society contrives to achieve poverty. Man's useful arts are all mere accelerations of nature ; if we can judge by his manner, Emerson here contemplates civilization not as a moral end or as a victory over barbarism, but as a final harmony with nature.

In the realms of the mind and the soul nature promises to be as all-sufficient as in the physical sphere. The eye is the first artist, the sunlight is the first painter. From them we learn the inner divine presence of beauty and the intellectual laws of æsthetics. The phenomena of matter turn themselves

into language for man to think and speak
with, and the world lends itself to be a
metaphor of the soul. Nature also disci-
plines the moral character, teaching us that
all debts must be paid by inexorable compensation, and gradually becoming man's sur-
rounding conscience, as it has become his
speech.

And lastly, nature teaches us that her life
is in the mind of man ; perhaps that is all
the life she has. She teaches us to understand God ; but what if she is only God's
process of teaching us, and does not exist
outside the process ? The more we understand her, the less real she seems and the
more real seem the laws she has taught. If
nature is our language, the means of external-
izing our thought, may she not be the exter-
nalization of divine thought in us, having
no other existence except as she is put forth
through us ?

The little book ends as it begins, with
insistence upon the dignity and self-sufficiency of the individual. No summary of
its ideas can reproduce the frequent rhapsody in which Emerson makes us see the
condition about which he is speculating. Like
all his later work, the book is persuasive by
its spirit rather than by its argument. The
individual sentences are brilliant, yet the
reader may wonder how he arrived from one

to another, or from paragraph to paragraph. It is this lack of constructive ability that has discredited Emerson with those readers who demand the step by step progress of well-reasoned science; it is for this that Thomas Hughes, otherwise well enough disposed to American literature, considered Emerson little better than a charlatan. But in the writing of his youth and middle age the logic is really there, though it remains an implication.

On August 31, 1837, Emerson delivered his Phi Beta Kappa address at Harvard, the famous essay on *The American Scholar*. The great success of that occasion, which in the opinion of many hearers was a veritable Independence Day for American scholarship, perhaps brought Emerson the invitation to address the Divinity School, July 15, 1838. The two speeches were but applications of one idea, the central theory of *Nature*— the idea that man, in order to be free, must cut loose from the past. In that lobe of its brain which attended to secular truth Harvard listened inspired while Emerson announced the time " when the sluggard intellect of this continent will look from under its iron lids, and fill the postponed expectation of the world with something better than the exertions of mechanical skill. Our day of dependence, our long apprenticeship to the

learning of other lands, draws to a close."
But a year later the theological part of the
Harvard mind recoiled in something like
horror from the statement that any tradition
of religion is worthless ; that Christianity
accepted on the teaching of another man,
even of a St. Paul, is not Christianity but
mere imitation ; that only he is religious who
discovers God in himself. The authorities
of the school disclaimed all responsibility
for such doctrine, and one of the professors
answered Emerson through a Boston paper.
Old Dr. Ware felt obliged to preach a ser-
mon on the situation, and sent it to his
former associate, and Emerson replied in a
letter of admirable temper. The incident
passed without any personal loss of affection,
though the Divinity School naturally looked
with suspicion upon Emerson for years.
Emerson, on his side, seems not to have
realized that his doctrine, sweeping away a
long-cherished idea of Christ and of God
was altogether out of place in a Christian
pulpit. For most of his life, however, he
gave up church-going, since the preaching
was not what he believed to be true, but he
liked his own children to go, and in his last
years he resumed the habit.

Meanwhile the secular lecturing and the
quiet Concord life continued, and the intellectual ferment then in progress in that part

of New England was taking the form of concrete experiments, with all of which Emerson was to some degree connected. The Transcendental Club was founded at the home of Mr. George Ripley, of Boston, September 19, 1836, for the purpose of discussing pressing topics of philosophy and religion. The meetings of the club took the form of " conversations," in which, of course, the readiest talker was likely to have the lion's share. Bronson Alcott and Margaret Fuller shone in these gatherings, as well as the radical and scholarly theologian, Theodore Parker (1810-1860); Emerson seems to have been, at least at first, chiefly a sympathetic listener. The group of friends at length determined to publish a magazine in the interest of their common ideals,—or perhaps it would be fairer to say, in the interest of the common spirit in which they pursued ideals. This paper, called *The Dial*, was issued quarterly from July, 1840, to April, 1844. Ripley at first looked after the publishing, and Margaret Fuller was the literary editor, with some aid from Emerson. In 1842 Emerson had to come to the rescue and assume full control, and Miss Peabody, Hawthorne's sister-in-law, sold the magazine. Some of the editing in the last two years, especially when Emerson had lecture engagements, was done by Thoreau, whom

Emerson admired in spite of Miss Fuller's disapproval. They three, with Alcott, were the most distinguished contributors; many of Emerson's poems were first printed in *The Dial*, and some of his lectures.

A more ambitious output of Transcendentalism was the Brook Farm experiment, which in point of date overlaps the publication of the magazine. In the conversations of the club there had been much discussion of ideal communities, until several of the younger spirits, notably George Ripley and W. H. Channing, were determined to found such a community. Emerson was busy with *The Dial* at the time, but he would have advised against the project in any circumstances, for with all the vagueness of his philosophy he was shrewd in practical concerns. He had not expected *The Dial* to succeed, and he saw still less hope for Ripley's scheme. But the scheme was put to the test; early in 1841 a milk-farm of one hundred and seventy acres was bought in West Roxbury for ten thousand five hundred dollars (£2,100), and mortgaged for six thousand dollars. A stock company was formed, and twenty-four shares of five hundred dollars each were taken by ten subscribers. Hawthorne, as we have seen, invested in two of these shares, and was made one of the financial directors of the company—from which circumstance it will be easily deduced that the management was hardly expert.

The aim of Brook Farm was " to insure a more natural union between intellectual and manual labour than now exists ; to combine the thinker and the worker, as far as possible, in the same individual ; to guarantee the highest mental freedom by providing all with labour adapted to their tastes and talents, and securing to them the fruits of their industry ; to do away with the necessity of menial services by opening the benefits of education and the profits of labour to all ; and thus to prepare a society of liberal, intelligent, cultivated persons, whose relations with each other would permit a more wholesome and simple life than can be led against the pressure of our competitive institutions." This was the form in which some of the Transcendentalists cared to emphasize their ideals. Margaret Fuller joined the experiment, and the hope of establishing such a community persisted in Alcott even after this experiment failed ; Hawthorne represented the type of Transcendentalist who was persuaded into the scheme and gradually lost his faith in it ; Emerson disapproved from the beginning. No plan for social betterment in which the essential was an adjustment of machinery could win his confidence. The Brook Farm experiment was finally abandoned in 1847.

Its end was probably hastened by the revising of its constitution in 1844 so as to include some features of Fourierism, which at that time was viewed with great suspicion.

Throughout this period of his life Emerson was busy lecturing. Almost all his prose-work was first seasoned in the lyceum courses before it got permanently into print. For this lecturing the pay was not very large. Emerson said that the most he had ever received was five hundred and seventy dollars (£114) for a series of ten lectures. In Boston he usually received fifty dollars for a lecture ; in the country districts ten dollars and travelling expenses. Such meagre profits from his work made continuous writing and travelling necessary. These lectures were published as *Essays* in two series, the first in 1841, the second in 1844. It is in these volumes that Emerson's Transcendentalism is most often studied. There the germs that were in *Nature* have expanded and ripened. and the spirit has changed ; instead of the early poetic rhapsody there is experience of the world and shrewd wit. Some of the essays, such as those on *Self-Reliance* and *Compensation*, are the wisest things Emerson wrote.

The philosophic scheme which conditions these writings, rather than appears explicitly in them, begins with the doctrine of the Over-Soul, which is, as it were, the concluding discovery of *Nature*. The Over-Soul is our higher self, our share in the infinite, God. When we are receptive to it, it possesses us, so to speak. Possessing us through the intellect, it is genius ; possessing us through the will, it is virtue ; possessing us through the affections, it is love. To be receptive to this Over-Soul, we must be in the most expansive state of freedom, and we arrive at that supreme condition only in solitude, for in society the past imprisons us. From the self-sufficiency of the soul, implied in these ideas, Emerson deduced his favourite doctrine of uncompromising self-reliance ; from the unity of all men in the Over-Soul, he deduced the opposing doctrine of companionableness and friendship. The use of friends is to recognize at fortunate moments in them, as in nature, some harmony between our better selves and the Over-Soul.

Prefaced to these essays Emerson published short poems as texts, often containing in concise form the essence of the prose. In 1846 he issued his first volume of poems, and a second collection in 1867. Splendid as some of the poems are in their ideal elevation or in their truth to his character, appreciation of them is largely an acquired taste. They are never song-like ; Emerson is a thinker, not a bard. He recognized some

prosaic incrustation of his nature, through
which his poetic yearning never got a clear
outlet. He is more successful in short pieces,
and in short passages from the longer poems,
and best of all in single immortal lines.

In October, 1847, Emerson made his
second visit to England and France, this
time for the purpose of lecturing in England.
The experience was memorable for the kindness with which he was everywhere received.
The *Essays* had been published in England
as soon as they appeared in America, and the
reading public were prepared to listen to
a prophet. The less initiated audiences were
somewhat dazed upon their first acquaintance with Emerson's Transcendentalism, but
his personality won them, as it had won
American audiences outside of New England.
Perhaps the best accounts of his manner as a
lecturer are to be got from the English impressions of him—of his fine voice, his natural
bearing, his sincere indifference to applause,
his elevation of soul. Among the literary
folk he made many friends, and he persuaded
Clough, somewhat later, to go to America.

This trip, which ended in July, 1848,
furnished him with the materials for *English
Traits*, 1856. Before that he had published
Representative Men, 1850, which classes itself
with Carlyle's *Heroes and Hero Worship*,
different as the books are in doctrine; and

in 1860 appeared *The Conduct of Life*. From this later year dates the financial success of Emerson's writings. All these books, even *English Traits*, are restatements or applications of the ideas in the *Essays* and in *Nature*. The remainder of his life contributed nothing essentially new to his work, but he lived in increasing honour, conscious of the best success. In his last years a loss of memory rendered his other faculties practically useless. He died at Concord, April 27, 1882.

The Transcendentalist who stood nearest to Emerson was Henry David Thoreau, whose reputation not improbably will finally equal or surpass Emerson's. It has long been his fortune to be known by only one book ; but now that his whole work is available in his journals, the vigour of his intellect is likely to get its long-delayed acknowledgment. And if we should compare the influence of any one of Emerson's books with the influence of *Walden* upon thought in America and Europe, the result would show in Thoreau an astonishing power of fertilizing other minds. His Transcendentalism is more practical, his thinking generally more solid, than Emerson's, and in scholarship he was Emerson's superior. That he has enjoyed a certain obscurity is due to his own indifference to the public, not to any lack of appreciation on the part of Emerson or his other friends.

He was born in Concord, July 12, 1817.
His father was a very skilful French pencil-
maker; his mother was a Scotch woman.
He had his education at the Concord Academy,
and at Harvard, where he was in residence
from 1833 to 1837. He then tried school-
teaching, and had the school at Concord
for two years, but gave it up finally because
the school board believed in flogging the
pupils and he did not. His singularly sweet
temper was by this time recognized in the
village, as well as his genius as a naturalist;
but he was also known to be self-reliant to
the point of eccentricity. He left old Dr.
Ripley's church in 1838, and refused to pay
the church tax. Having mastered his father's
craft, and having won praise in Boston for
making the best pencil in America, he announced to his astonished friends that he
would never make another pencil; why
should he repeat his work? He solved the
problem of living, not by earning money,
but by learning to do without non-essentials,
believing that " a man is rich in proportion
to the number of things he can do without."
When he did need money, he worked at
anything that offered itself at the moment;
and as he was a master carpenter, mason,
pencil-maker, and numerous other things,
and as one occupation was to him as honourable as another, he had no difficulty in

I

providing for himself. The various engagements necessary for his support came to
about six weeks' work every year; the rest
of his time he was free.

In 1838 he tried lecturing, and spoke on
Society at Concord; but for such work he
had no gifts. At this time he became intimate with Emerson and the other Transcendentalists; and from 1841 to 1843 he lived in
the Emerson household, partly because Emerson wanted his comradeship, and partly to
look after the house when Emerson was away
lecturing. He next did some tutoring in the
family of William Emerson, then living at
Staten Island, New York, and in 1845 he
lived in his famous seclusion on Emerson's
property at Walden Pond. The attempt at
Brook Farm to perfect man in the community
suggested to Thoreau the opposite experiment of perfecting man in solitude. In 1847
he returned to his father's home in Concord,
and the results of his experiment are recorded
in his famous book, *Walden*, 1854.

While he was living at Walden Pond he
suffered imprisonment for refusing to pay
his war tax. He did not believe in the
Mexican War, and felt bound in conscience
not to assist it. After expostulating with
him, the authorities felt equally bound in
conscience to lock him up. He was arrested
as he came into Concord for a pair of shoes

left at the shoemaker's. That night he passed in the jail with great serenity of mind, even good humour. The occasion was memorable for his significant retort to Emerson, who had come to see what was wrong. "Why are you in there, David?" asked Emerson. "Ralph, why are you outside?" was the reply. The next morning Thoreau was furiously angry to find that his family had paid his tax for him. As there was no help for it, however, he recovered his poise, accepted his freedom, and continued his way to the shoemaker's.

Thoreau's doctrine and practice of the simple life was bound up with his love of nature, which differed from that of Wordsworth and Emerson in that it was more definitely scientific. His first book, *A Week on the Concord*, 1849, had failed, perhaps because that kind of nature-worship was somewhat beyond the average untrained citizen. As he grew older Thoreau became parochial in enthusiasm; for him nature came to mean Concord; when he read a book on the Arctic regions, he took delight in saying that almost all the phenomena there described could be observed in Concord.

The end of his not very long life was most honourable, not only because of the steadily accumulating respect of his integrity, but because of his heroic and eloquent defence of John Brown. Concord did not approve of Brown's raid, although the abolitionist sentiment there was strong. Therefore, Thoreau knew that he was braving public sentiment when he determined to plead for the man then on trial for his life. He invited all Concord to the meeting house on a Sunday evening to hear his plea for Brown. Emerson and other friends tried to dissuade him, but he persisted, and for once the power of his feelings made him an eloquent lecturer. The audience listened in silence, but with sympathy, and he was asked to repeat the address elsewhere.

The last important moment of this solitary life was, therefore, in a social setting, in an act of what he deemed to be public service. His health had already become a matter of concern, and he died of consumption, May 6, 1862.

Thoreau's writing usually takes the form of a journal, in which the thread of narrative bears this resemblance to the thread of argument in Emerson—that its chief interest lies in the descriptions and meditations which interrupt it. In these passages Thoreau reveals a character of great sanity, with gifts of positive realism and a wealth of sense not often associated with the idealizing faculty. He is not a dreamer, but an observer, his vision is both thoughtful and poetic, but he looks steadily at life.

The third in importance of the Transcendentalists is Sarah Margaret Fuller, born in Cambridgeport, May 23, 1810. Her father, who was a lawyer of some importance in public life, tried to give her a precocious education, and only partly succeeded, but the attempt ruined her health. He died when she was twenty-five years old, and she was forced to care for her family. After some teaching in Alcott's school and elsewhere, she settled near Boston, conducted " conversations " in the Transcendentalist fashion, and won recognition, more by conversation than by writing, as a literary critic. Her personality seems to have been strangely inspiring, although she was not attractive in appearance, and the secret of her charm is lost. But her knowledge of Greek and German literature would have been almost enough, even without her powers of inspiration, to set her far above the incompetent American criticism of her time. She was the literary leader of Transcendentalism, and the natural editor for *The Dial*, in which much of her best writing appeared. Probably she will hold her place longest with a few of her poems, but her critical service was great at the time ; she introduced Goethe into New England, for example, much as Emerson there introduced Carlyle.

Miss Fuller travelled much in America,

was for a while literary editor of the *New York Tribune*, under Horace Greeley, and spent some years abroad. It is, perhaps, not the least of her achievements that she was the only prominent Transcendentalist who found Concord and its neighbourhood somewhat parochial. She preferred Italy, for example. In 1847 she secretly married Giovanni Angelo, Marquis Ossoli, and a son was born in 1848. In May, 1850, she started for America with her husband and child; but after a long voyage the vessel was wrecked on Fire Island, July 19, and the family were all drowned. A collected edition of her writings appeared in 1855.

Amos Bronson Alcott was perhaps more nearly the fountain head of Transcendentalism than Emerson; but his influence was unliterary, and in a record of American literature he stands much below the three writers already treated. He was born in Connecticut, November 29, 1799. His youth was spent in various attempts at industry, in all of which he demonstrated his sorry proportion of practical sense to fine ideals. In his twenty-seventh year he settled into school teaching, and developed ideas of pedagogy far in advance of his time. These ideas he put into practice in his famous school, founded at Boston in 1834. The institution failed, however, after a brilliant promise of success, and with his family Alcott removed to Concord. The second of his daughters, Louise May Alcott (1832-1888), described the family habit of plain living and high thinking in *Little Women*, 1867.

Alcott's service to American literature is chiefly as an inspirer of Emerson. His *Orphic Sayings*, contributed to *The Dial*, have little value apart from the general movement of Transcendentalism. His attempt to start a community, " Fruitlands," after Brook Farm had failed, was only another illustration of how impervious his ideals were to experience. The remainder of his life he occupied himself with his lectures or " conversations," at which kind of expression he excelled all the other Transcendentalists. Impractical and even ridiculous as he could sometimes be, the testimony to his nobility of spirit and inspiration is too unanimous to be disregarded. His fame rests chiefly on that testimony, and on his reports of his pedagogical ideas. He died March 4, 1888, having lived to see himself the patron saint and thinker of the Concord School of Philosophy. With the poets Christopher Cranch, Jones Very, and Ellery Channing, with George Ripley, the critic, with numerous lecturers and preachers of the period, with philosophers like the elder

Henry James, with the novelist Sylvester Judd, he remains to the student a figure of interest not untouched by pathos, but to the large public scarcely more than a name.

CHAPTER VII

THE NEW ENGLAND POETS

DURING the thirty years that preceded the
Civil War, New England became once more
the literary centre of America, and the period
may be called with no great exaggeration
the Golden Age of American Literature. The
greatest poets, the greatest prose romancer,
the greatest philosopher, the greatest interpreter of nature, the greatest orator, and the
greatest historians all belonged to the small
region which had declined in political influence,
but had increased its wealth, improved its
educational facilities, and retained much of
its homogeneity of character. Boston and
Cambridge were the centre of the region's
literary and spiritual activity, and although
it is in some respects ridiculous to speak of the
first of these cities as the Athens of America,
there is more excuse for the phrase than
appears at first thought. Boston, like Athens,
was the capital of a comparatively small,
homogeneous, alert people, and it was a
centre of creative energy in thought and in
at least one branch of art.

Of all the New Englanders who during this period laid the enduring foundations of American Literature, by far the most popular and perhaps the most influential—save possibly Emerson—was Henry Wadsworth Longfellow, the poet who shared with Tennyson the allegiance of the Anglo-Saxon world during a large part of the last century. He was born of exceptionally good stock on February 27, 1807, at Portland, Maine, a city which only the year before had been the birthplace of a small poet and prolific journalist, Nathaniel Parker Willis (1806-1867), whose once brilliant fame has suffered a not altogether merited eclipse. Longfellow did not, like Willis, attain notoriety too suddenly ; and although he too spent some time in travel, he did not, like Willis, expatriate himself for a while or leave New England to reside in the more cosmopolitan and turbulent New York. The younger of the two Portland boys doubtless had the deeper and the quieter nature. He was always a lover of the sea, and later he expressed some of its power and charm in his poetry. As a boy, also, and as a college student at Bowdoin, he yielded himself to the fascination of books, with the result that he became one of the most important transmitters of old-world culture to his provincial countrymen. Such a youth was sure to write verses early, and some of his juvenile poetry was praised in an absurd way, which, fortunately, did not turn his head.

On the whole, Longfellow's life was uneventful, and save for two bereavements, singularly free from strain and care. He was offered a professorship of modern languages in his *alma mater*, and was enabled to spend three years in Europe in preparation for its duties. On his return he became a good teacher, wrote some modest text-books, and contributed reviews and sketches of travel to periodicals. A collection of his sketches and tales was published in 1835 under the title of *Outre-Mer: A Pilgrimage beyond the Sea*. In other words, he was still at twenty-eight a rather callow and sentimental follower of Irving. About this time he received a call to the chair which the far more scholarly Ticknor was relinquishing at Harvard; and he sailed with his young wife on another voyage for Europe in quest of culture. His wife died in Holland, and grief for her opened his heart to the influence of German sentiment, as is shown by his prose romance *Hyperion* and by some of his poems. He returned to America late in 1836, and filled his chair at Harvard acceptably until he retired in 1854. He had long found his duties irksome, partly because too much drudgery was laid upon him, partly because his bent was that of the poet rather than that of the teacher or scholar. Yet one scarcely sympathizes with the complaints he utters in his diary, for he was most comfortably established in the well-known Craigie House, he made an exceptionally happy second marriage, he enjoyed much congenial society, and he was the most popular poet of his day. Ever since 1839, when he published *Voices of the Night* containing the *Psalm of Life* and other pieces admirably adapted to the spiritual aspirations of his countrymen, and not too sophisticated in style to answer their simple demands in matters of æsthetics, he had been the recipient of a blended admiration and esteem more wide spread and genuine than falls to the lot of any save the most favoured of mortals. Longfellow was not favoured with exceptional genius, as poetical genius is usually appraised ; but few writers have been more felicitously endowed with that power of interpreting a people's heart which wins for him who exerts it unmeretricious fame.

It would be out of place to attempt to give a list of Longfellow's volumes of poetry, or to dwell upon his sporadic attempts to win favour by his prose. With his early volumes he made himself popular by such pieces as *The Village Blacksmith* and *Excelsior*, but he also won favour from more critical

readers by the rhythmical mastery and the
romantic spirit to be found in such a ballad
as *The Skeleton in Armour*. Apparently he
owed more to German poetry than he did
to English romantic poets such as Keats
and Coleridge, a fact in which we may find
a partial explanation of his appeal to the
general public and of his failure to satisfy
exigent latter-day readers. Perhaps when
critics and poets acquire greater catholicity
of taste, his simple narrative and reflective
poems will be more fully appreciated. In
the more elaborate forms of poetry, or, if
one will, the more artificial forms, his success,
save in his sonnets, some of which are admirable, was never very marked. He could impart charm to *The Golden Legend of* 1851,
based upon Hartmann von Aue's *Der Arme
Heinrich;* but when later he added to this
The Divine Tragedy and *The New England
Tragedies* in order to make up his ambitious
poem *Christus*, he failed completely to attract
any class of readers. He had no dramatic
genius, and his real story-telling gifts did not
move at an epic level. Hence it was fortunate
for him that Hawthorne gave him the theme
of the pathetic idyll *Evangeline*, which in 1847
set the seal upon his popularity, and that in
Hiawatha and *The Courtship of Miles Standish*
he found subjects which both satisfied readers
who demanded poetry based upon the past of

America and suited his own genuine but far from lofty powers. As he was not a master of blank verse, he was wise in adopting for these poems exotic measures—hexameters and rhymeless trochaic tetrameters—whatever may be thought of the amount of profit his innovations are likely to afford to other poets. *The Courtship of Mile Standish*, perhaps the least facile and most authentically American of his ambitious poems, is good enough to give its author a high rank among modern narrative poets ; and there are several pieces to be found in the *Tales of a Wayside Inn* that almost justify the belief that Longfellow's gifts as a story-teller constitute the best basis for his fame.

A little reflection, however, causes one to doubt whether even the still popular *Evangeline* and *Hiawatha*, which are studied in American schools, or such spirited poems as *Paul Revere's Ride* and *The Saga of King Olaf* are likely to wear as well in the centuries to come as the small group of reflective lyrics, such as *The Bridge* and *The Day is Done*, in which Longfellow makes a sweet, simple appeal to the universal heart of man. He was a master of pensive sentiment, which he expressed in stanzas whose art is as unobtrusive as it is adequate, being neither sophisticated nor crude. What can be better in their way than these lines from *The Bridge?*

" And I think how many thousands
    Of care-encumbered men,
  Each bearing his burden of sorrow,
    Have crossed the bridge since then.

" I see the long procession
    Still passing to and fro,
  The young heart hot and restless,
    And the old subdued and slow !

" And forever and forever,
    As long as the river flows,
  As long as the heart has passions,
    As long as life has woes,

" The moon and its broken reflection
    And its shadows shall appear,
  As the symbol of love in heaven,
    And its wavering image here."

What the poet who could write thus
suffered when in July, 1861, his charming
wife was accidently burned to death, can be
imagined rather than described. He survived her until March 24, 1882, and about
four years before he died he wrote upon his
great bereavement a beautiful sonnet, *The
Cross of Snow*. As a solace he undertook a
translation of *The Divine Comedy*, which,
despite a certain facility, has received high
praise. He had long before shown himself
to be an excellent translator of German
lyrics ; and, as has already been said, not the
least of his claims upon the gratitude of

Americans is the service he rendered throughout his life as a transmitter of European culture. He deserved amply the blended love and homage paid him during his declining years ; and it would seem that he deserves, now that sufficient time has been allowed for the detraction that usually follows a writer's death, a less grudging acknowledgment of his unspectacular but sterling merits than is awarded him by would-be representatives of aristocratic taste. If one were certain that the contemners of Longfellow spent most of their time with Sophocles and Milton, one could bear with more equanimity their efforts to disparage one of the truest poets and, within limits, most accomplished artists America has produced.

John Greenleaf Whittier, although in some respects a more influential poet than Longfellow, never attained the latter's popularity. He, too, was born in 1807—on December 17—and he also represented good New England stock, but a stock quite different from that of the Longfellows. His parents were Quakers who lived at East Haverhill, Massachusetts, where his father was a small farmer. The boy inherited their primitive virtues, and grew up amid straitened circumstances faithfully described in the best of his sustained poems, the idyll entitled *Snow-Bound*. He got little schooling, but he read a few good books and showed capacity for writing verses. Some of his poems were published in a neighboring newspaper and brought Whittier to the notice of its editor, William Lloyd Garrison, who urged that the young farm labourer should be sent back to school. This advice was followed as far as was practicable, and then, for a while, Whittier secured employment as a journalist at Boston. He later returned to the paternal farm, but after his father's death he tried journalism in Hartford until he was forced by feeble health to return home. He had managed to make not a little local reputation for himself as a versifier, and he had begun to take a strong interest in politics. In 1833 he published a pamphlet, *Justice and Expediency*, which aligned him with the Abolitionists, and made a conspicuous career of office-holding impossible. One can hardly regret that Whittier became a sort of Tyrtaeus, instead of a Whig politician and orator treading reverently in the footsteps of Henry Clay; nor can one fail to perceive that his knowledge of politics made the new anti-slavery advocate a less visionary leader than some of his fellow crusaders.

In 1836 Whittier removed to the village of Amesbury, where about four years later, after a brief and stormy experience as an anti-slavery editor in Philadelphia, he made his

K

permanent abode. Meanwhile he had published *Mogg Megone*, a poem on a colonial theme treated in the manner of Scott, and he had begun the stirring series of poems in behalf of freedom which is the chief basis of his fame. On the side of art, these early verses are immature and crude; but they make a manly appeal to the best in human nature, and it is no wonder that they were widely copied by the newspapers of the Free States They brought their author little money, however, and his feeble health prevented him from being active in more profitable ways; hence he lived in more or less restricted circumstances until 1866, the year in which the popular *Snow-Bound* was published. For some years he contributed frequently to the *New Era*, the periodical in which *Uncle Tom's Cabin* first appeared, and he did not confine himself to poetry, as the collected volumes of his prose works will prove to any one who will take the trouble to examine them. The prose of poets is usually good, and Whittier's prose is not a striking exception to the rule; but on the whole it has little vitality. It is as the Quaker Poet of Freedom, who helped to bring on the great contest over slavery, and during its progress, despite his honest advocacy of the peace dear to his sect, managed to encourage the North by patriotic

lyrics like *Barbara Frietchie*, that Whittier
has impressed himself upon the world; and
it is as a poet of human freedom that he must
live if he is to hold his own with posterity.
He has to his credit some good poetry descriptive of nature in New England; and at his
best he is a true poet of the domestic affections—witness the verses entitled *Memories*
—but his success in these attractive fields
is scarcely sufficiently conspicuous to support
the position he has held for two generations
in American literature.

In part this position is clearly due to Whittier's character, in part to the fact that he
long survived to receive the homage of the
New America that sprang into being after
the Civil War. He lived until September 7,
1892; and it seemed as if his tender heart,
denied the pleasure of lavishing itself upon
wife and children, had spent itself in affection
for country and mankind. He mellowed soon,
especially after the death of a favourite sister
and after the war had removed the hated
institution of slavery. No vindictiveness
toward old opponents marred his career, as
it did that of many a politician. The collections of verse that appeared with fair frequency
during his latter years might leave some doubt
of their author's high genius, but none of his
essential nobility.

How far his poetical works in their entirety

are read to-day, and with what feelings, it would be hard to say. His elaborate poems are few and unimportant ; his short poems are very numerous, amounting to several hundreds, and continually being increased by accessions from manuscript sources. From each of the chief divisions he adopted—the *Poems of Nature*, the *Ballads and Narrative Poems*, the *Personal Poems*, the *Anti-slavery Poems*, and the *Poems Subjective and Reminiscent*—anthologists and readers have selected pieces that in spirit and execution deserved sincere, though in but few cases perhaps enthusiastic, praise. But both in these chosen poems, such as *Maud Muller, Ichabod, Massachusetts to Virginia*, and *In Schooldays*, to name no others, and in the hundreds upon hundreds that remain one feels that Whittier was a poet by inspiration rather than a poet by inspiration and art combined. His emotional qualifications were of a high order ; and, although he was often careless in metrical and stylistic technique, he generally managed to attain a fair level of excellence. But, on the whole, he displayed no great strength of intellect or of imagination, and little of that marked individuality of temperament which in the opinion of many is the chief mark of genius. In other words, he not only, like most other poets, has a large mass of rather factitious, undistinguished work to carry in the revised edition of his poems ; but he has not a well-defined domain of mastery save, perhaps, in the verses inspired by the contest over slavery. These have a moral and an historical value that may long continue to lend them vitality ; but it is obvious that one could feel more convinced of Whittier's high and permanent importance as a poet if, like Longfellow, for example, he were conspicuously excellent as a narrative poet and made a special appeal through a group of reflective pieces to the universal heart of man. Partisan admiration such as Poe has secured is out of the question for him, and he makes no such appeal to the serious minded as does Emerson. His hold upon unsophisticated readers who are docile to tradition and full of patriotism has doubtless continued fairly strong, and the teaching of American literature in the schools will undoubtedly help to maintain his reputation ; but, when all is said, one is left wondering how the sophisticated public of two generations hence will regard him.

The future, however, does not concern us as much as the present, and there are many of Whittier's poems which repay a careful examination of his works and which, if published as a volume of winnowed selections, would go far toward justifying the opinion that none of the New England poets had a greater native endowment than he. Perhaps if he had had the early advantages of education granted to Longfellow and Lowell, or their opportunities of contact with the culture of the Old World, his art would have been refined without loss of strength and his imagination stimulated. Even as it is, few American poets have to their credit more lovely stanzas than those composing the *Proem* to the first general collection of his poems ; and no American poem of rural life forms a sweeter or sincerer idyll than *Snow-Bound*, despite the fact that it is couched in facile octosyllabics, and that it has few or no touches of high imaginative power. Its simplicity and tenderness have insured it greater consideration from Whittier's countrymen than it would have obtained had its strictly poetic merits been of higher order ; for, although a democratic public may be always trusted to seek the best, it does not always recognize it. No public, however, could have failed to be moved by such stirring occasional poems as *Randolph of Roanoke* and *Moloch in State Street*, or by not a few of his ballads, factitious though many of the latter class of poems may seem to be. Perhaps the greatest of all his poems is an occasional one—the short but terrible lament entitled *Ichabod*, written when that New England idol, Daniel Webster, had, in the eyes of the

anti-slavery men, fallen from his pedestal.
Here, for once, Whittier's art was flawless.
The stanzas fairly glow with repressed passion, and one feels that no apologist for
Webster, no matter how just his contention
that they do the great orator injustice, will
ever be able fully to counteract their deadly
effect. It is the irony of fate that a kindly
Quaker should have shown his highest reach
of poetic power in such a stinging stanza as

> ' All else is gone ; from those great eyes
> The soul has fled :
> When faith is lost, when honour dies,
> The man is dead."

The third of the New England group of
poets, Dr. Oliver Wendell Holmes, is probably most often thought of as the genial autocrat—that is, as a writer of prose. Holmes
was born at Cambridge, Massachusetts, on
August 29, 1809—the year of Lincoln and
Poe and of many other great men, not
Americans. He was the son of Dr. Abiel
Holmes, historian and divine, and he came
of true New England Brahmin stock. His
geniality and urbanity were in direct proportion with his calvinistic ancestors' sternness
and narrowness, and it is scarcely fanciful
to regard him as a changeling. It is certainly not fanciful to see in him one of the
most effective of the liberal spirits who in

the first half of the nineteenth century suc-
cessfully stormed the citadel of New England
orthodoxy. Stormed, however, is not the
right word, especially for Holmes. His work
was rather that of a sapper.

It was only natural that a Cambridge lad
should be sent to Harvard ; and at that
college Holmes graduated in the class of
1829, familiar to the reader of his long
series of class-reunion poems. His humour,
sentiment, and knowledge of the college traditions made him the ideal Harvard laureate,
but he would have been a good occasional
poet in any environment. He began writing
verse early, and the year after graduating
he attracted attention by a short poem
entitled *Old Ironsides,* in which he pleaded
for the preservation of the famous frigate
Constitution. Then he wrote what is perhaps the most perfect of his contributions
to society verse, *The Last Leaf,* and displayed
his skill in frankly comic productions. Later
attempts in more ambitious fields of poetry
were scarcely successful ; and it may be held
with some justice that he was as good a
poet in his youth as in his maturity and old
age. He was quick too, in displaying his
talents for the discursive conversational essay,
as is proved by the fact that in 1831 and 1832
he published in a magazine two papers entitled
The Autocrat of the Breakfast Table.

Despite this almost premature display of literary ability, he did not contemplate a strictly literary life, but studied medicine, first at Boston, then in Paris. On his return from Europe he practised his profession in Boston until 1847, when he accepted the chair of anatomy in Harvard, having previously filled the same post for a short time in another college. He had gained some distinction as a medical writer, had married, and had collected his poems in a volume to which he now furnished a companion. Both collections contained pieces of merit, but neither gave proof of much capacity in the higher types of imaginative poetry. Holmes was easily the best man to invite to prepare a poem to be read at a public dinner ; and no one could vie with him in producing polished heroic couplets of the sort that pleased eighteenth-century ears. But he was writing for a public that had become acquainted with Wordsworth, Coleridge, Byron, Shelley, and Keats, and that was beginning to admire Tennyson and Longfellow. Hence, although he attained a good reputation as a poet, particularly in New England, he made no profound appeal to any class of readers, and he would probably never have risen to be included among the major American authors had he not, when nearly fifty, taken up his early dropped rôle of gracious and wise essayist. Whether, when we become able to judge romantic poets and critics with some sort of sanity, and to redress some of the wrongs they have done to the poets of the eighteenth century, we shall read the poetry of Holmes in mass with much greater pleasure than we do now, may be doubted—much of it is too factitious and thin—but, perhaps, we shall do greater justice to the taste which impelled the good Doctor to abide by the classic style of his predecessors, and we may be able better to understand and appreciate the attempts he made to defend his favorite poetic measure.

Holmes filled his Harvard chair from 1847 to 1882, and was a faithful and successful teacher. One at least of his contributions to medical literature is acknowledged to be of importance ; and it is a comfort to think that he can be added to the roll of men of genius who have had a good deal of method without any madness. There might have been some question of his genius, however, had not a fortunate event happened just ten years after he entered upon his duties at Harvard. This was the founding of the *Atlantic Monthly* at Boston in 1857—a magazine destined to be the most important of American literary periodicals, coming as it did after the genius of the country had been liberated in New England during the period of Transcendentalist and Anti-slavery activity. Lowell, the editor of the new monthly, applied to Holmes for contributions ; and the latter recalled the articles he had written as " Autocrat " twenty-five years before for an earlier organ of New England culture. It was not exactly the case of another Scott finding the forgotten manuscript of the beginning of *Waverley ;* but it was an auspicious turning-point in the life of Holmes the author, and in time it gave to America what bids fair to remain for a considerable period one of its prose classics. The new Autocrat was no longer a youth of premature genius, but a mellowed man of nearly fifty, whose experience had given him insight into life and character, yet had increased rather than diminished his native geniality and tenderness of spirit. He could now be wise as well as humourous, he could display a mild skill in creating characters, he could go his own way and gait—certain that he had begun adequately to express his own genius, and to make an individual appeal to the public heart.

The Autocrat of the Breakfast Table appeared as a book in 1858, and *The Professor at the Breakfast Table* in 1860. The increased element of fiction in the second and less notable volume served to introduce the now fairly active writer to an expectant public as a novelist. *Elsie Venner,* his first and best

novel, appeared in 1861, and in the same year
he issued another collection of poems. The
novel showed that its author had abandoned
his true province, yet, as not infrequently
happens, it proved that the work of a man of
real genius is likely to be memorable for one
reason or another, no matter what the field
of his activity. Holmes might not have the
narrative skill requisite to the production
of fiction of the first order ; but he was still
able to use his gifts as an observer, he was
still a kindly humourist, and he had chosen
a subject congenial to a physician with a
scientific bent. Some have found the story
of his snake-like heroine too repulsive, but
even these persons must have enjoyed his
pictures of New England village life. Later
realists have given us more carefully finished
pictures, but Holmes has in *Elsie Venner*
one great advantage over most of his modern
rivals. The queer uncanniness of his book
gives it a unique and memorable quality
that has, as it were, niched it in the popular
mind. Most realistic work, no matter how
perfect, tends to take its unremembered
place in a sort of photograph album of fiction of which we rarely turn the leaves.
In such an album, it is to be feared, some
of us have put away Holmes's other novels,
The Guardian Angel of 1867 and *A Mortal
Antipathy* of 1885. Yet the former of these

like *Elsie Venner*, has an abnormal theme, displays its author's special gifts, and is worth reading both by the admirer of Holmes and by the general reader.

The books of Holmes's old age doubtless helped to make it green and introduced him to new readers, while enabling him to maintain his hold upon the affections of friends he had made in his youth and in his prime. There is no need, however, to dwell upon them here. He posed as the Poet at the Breakfast Table, and he was his gracious self. Over the teacups, he described a short tour in Europe, he issued volumes of verses—often memorial, for he was surviving his friends—he collected his miscellaneous essays, he tried his hand at biography, and then, full of years and honours, he died at Boston on October 7, 1894, the most distinguished and representative Bostonian and one of the truest and best loved Americans of his long day.

As has been sufficiently indicated, his rank as a poet is not a very high one, but his admirers may well reply that it makes little difference whether so delightful a poet, so complete a master of familiar verse, is great or minor. The fame of the author of *The Last Leaf*, of *Dorothy Q*, of *The Chambered Nautilus*, of *The Deacon's Masterpiece* is as secure in the hearts of his readers as that of any of his American contemporaries of wider art and deeper emotional appeal. Just so, there are people who read Matthew Prior oftener than they do Alfred Tennyson, and who will not apologize to anyone for their preference. But Prior is not by any means so great a poet as Tennyson; and Holmes cannot well be ranked with Longfellow and Whittier and Lowell, or even with that master in the narrow vein, Edgar Allan Poe. What matter! He wrote the stanza

> "And if I should live to be
> The last leaf upon the tree
>   In the spring,
> Let them smile as I do now,
> At the old forsaken bough
>   Where I cling."

He wrote also

> "Grandmother's mother: her age I guess,
> Thirteen summers, or something less;
> Girlish bust, but womanly air;
> Smooth, square forehead with uprolled hair;
> Lips that lover has never kissed;
> Taper fingers and slender wrist;
> Hanging sleeves of stiff brocade;
> So they painted the little maid."

He wrote also in higher mood

> "Build thee more stately mansions, O my soul,
>   As the swift seasons roll!
>   Leave thy low-vaulted past!
> Let each new temple, nobler than the last,
> Shut thee from heaven with a dome more vast,
>   Till thou at length art free,
> Leaving thine outgrown shell by life's unresting sea."

The future will winnow Holmes's prose as carefully as it will his verses; and it may be that only a small collection of choice passages —reduced essays let us call them—will be left. Certainly most of his fairly numerous volumes of prose will stand for longer and longer periods unopened on our shelves, and perhaps they will steadily move up to higher shelves. But one does not like to think of *The Autocrat of the Breakfast Table* and *Elsie Venner*, at least of the original " Autocrat," undergoing this upward migration.

The fourth of the chief poets of New England, James Russell Lowell, was born at Cambridge on February 22, 1819, nearly ten years after Holmes. He, too, was of Brahmin stock and thoroughly representative of Harvard—in the matter of scholarship and wide culture more representative than Holmes. He graduated in 1838, after some escapades, and in his class poem he gave early proof of his satiric powers. He was admitted to the bar, but showed no signs of desiring to practise law, the writing of verses being a more delightful occupation, one followed by the charming girl Maria White, to whom he was finally married in 1844. It is needless to name or discuss his first volumes of poetry, which showed the influence of Keats, or to dwell upon his attempt to start a magazine, or to comment upon his interesting beginnings as a prose critic. Many of the best characteristics of the mature man were observable in the attractive young poet, but he was, perhaps, somewhat slow in finding himself. Fortunately he never gave himself completely over to Transcendentalism, although impelled in that direction by his idealistic wife. She stimulated his love of freedom, a fact not without its influence upon his later career, when both in prose and in verse he voiced the best political aspirations of his countrymen. Important also in this respect was his service on an anti-slavery paper in Philadelphia ; and even if his early reviews, poems, and political articles are of but the very slightest value to-day, they helped to make Lowell the most broadly accomplished and one of the most practically influential of American writers.

The Lowell we know first emerges in his racy dialect poems known as *The Biglow Papers*, which began in the *Boston Courier* in June, 1846. In 1848 the first series of these humourous and satiric poems, the best of their kind in American literature, appeared in book form ; the second series followed during the Civil War and, although in some respects less successful than the series dealing with politics during the war with Mexico, was worthy of its author's reputation and of the great crisis that called it forth. In the first series Lowell's strictly creative genius is probably seen at its height. Elsewhere in his verse he is in continual danger of suggesting the work or the manner of other poets; here he is to all intents and purposes an original master. His rustics are real human beings who discuss contemporary politics in the best Yankee dialect. For wit and wisdom, for keen political intelligence, for honest hatred of shams and deep sympathy with what is best in life, for satiric power that can not merely sting and lash but fairly sweep away, these poems are unique and worthy of high praise. Their appeal to-day is probably limited in the main to readers who know something of American history, and the satirist who now desires to influence public opinion is almost certain to employ prose and to dispense with Lowell's learning; but then the modern satirist is not likely to come as near as Lowell did to producing a classic.

The year of the first series of *The Biglow Papers* also saw the publication of two of Lowell's most popular and sustained poems, *The Vision of Sir Launfal* and *A Fable for Critics*. Neither is a masterpiece, but both furnish good evidence of his versatility and power. The former has retained its popularity better than the latter, a fact which is not surprising since the one poem is a senti-

L

mental and highly moral piece of modernized
Arthurian romance introduced by some charming verses in praise of June, while the other
is a satire which concerns itself in part with
small and long-forgotten authors. Yet the
exuberant genius of Lowell is really more
manifest in the less remembered poem,
which is one of the best of its kind. In some
respects, of course, *A Fable for Critics* is
derivative ; it plainly belongs to a group of
anapæstic *jeux d'esprit*, of which the earliest
important example is Suckling's *Session of
the Poets*. But Lowell's overflowing humour
was his own, and so was his generous praise
of all the contemporaries for whose productions he could feel any genuine admiration.
Perhaps he was too generous, but that is a
good fault. He certainly displayed modera-
tion in his satire upon the poor poets of the
period, who were wretched enough to justify
the indignation of a Dryden and the spleen
of a Pope, as anyone may convince himself
who will examine carefully the Reverend
Rufus Wilmot Griswold's portentous anthology of 1842 entitled *Poets and Poetry of
America*. Both this volume and Lowell's
half-panegyrical, half-satiric poem are emin-
ently representative of the period and of the
democracy that produced them. The period
swarmed with mediocre writers which the
democracy knew no better than to tolerate.

Yet, after all, who that has seen a democracy roused to blind anger will wish to see it anything but kindly—even to bad poets. A *Fable for Critics* is a better model for our future satirists than *The Dunciad*.

Lowell entered the third decade of his life with a reputation which a more strictly professional writer would easily and speedily have enhanced. That he did not greatly increase it for some years seems to have been due in part to his domestic circumstances. His wife was frail, they had lost children, and a change of scene seemed needed. In July, 1851, they sailed to Italy and remained abroad fifteen months, the visit being of great service to a man whose mind was so open to impressions and whose love of culture was so genuine. A year after his return his wife died, and he was left to care for a little daughter. He wrote some verse and prose full of a true feeling for nature ; and he lectured on poetry so acceptably that he was offered the chair at Harvard that Longfellow had resigned. After another journey to Europe he entered with success upon his professional duties, in which he displayed great geniality as a teacher and broad attainments as a scholar. In 1857 he made a fortunate second marriage, and as editor of *The Atlantic Monthly* put that periodical upon the path of success. After four years the *Monthly* passed into other hands, and Lowell was free to express his thoughts and feelings about the great civil struggle that had begun. The second series of the *Biglow Papers* has been mentioned ; but undoubtedly his greatest poem of the period is the *Commemoration Ode* recited in 1865 at the ceremonies at Harvard in honour of the alumni who had fallen in the war. This and Lowell's other odes, particularly that written ten years later for the hundredth anniversary of Washington's taking command of the American army, constitute probably the chief basis for the admiration of those readers —and there are such—who regard Lowell as the best of American poets. They are, indeed, poems of high excellence such as none but a true poet of trained powers could have composed, and they make, in passages, a splendid appeal to American patriotism. They are diffuse, however, and, in the opinion of some, fall below Lowell's greatest models in perfect flawlessness of poetic art, being in some respects too subtle and unspontaneous. Indeed, it is difficult not to feel that Lowell's later poems, as one reads them in their collected form, especially in the collections of 1868 and 1888, fall short in range, copiousness, and originality of genius, of what might have been expected of a poet endowed with his powers, ideals, and opportunities. He never quite touches the heart as Longfellow does ; he has not the individual quality so notable in Emerson, Poe, and Whitman. But he was the most cultured of American poets, and in the *Biglow Papers* a master in his way.

Meanwhile Lowell had been joint-editor with Professor Charles Eliot Norton of the old *North American Review*, and had contributed to it some noteworthy political and literary articles. He also showed his genius as a true essayist in such pieces as *My Garden Acquaintance* and *On a Certain Condescension in Foreigners*. His collected papers, *Among My Books* of 1870 and *My Study Windows* of 1871, proved him to be easily the most scholarly and readable of American critics. It was no great task to eclipse his predecessors, save Poe, and his contemporaries ; but the praise just given him holds true of him even after the lapse of forty years and after a marked improvement in the general quality of American criticism. Indeed, by 1870, the year of the publication of that over-rated poem *The Cathedral*, inspired by the beautiful edifice at Chartres, Lowell had made himself the greatest of American men of letters, the writer one naturally puts in rivalry with Matthew Arnold. We need not compare them here, but may venture the remark that, good as Lowell is in such critical essays as those on Chaucer and Dryden, he is not the master of a critical method which can be more or less applied by others. His chief faults as a critic are, perhaps, due in large measure to two characteristics that make him delightful as a writer—his independence and his ebullient humour.

In 1872 Lowell gave up his professorship at Harvard, and went abroad for two years. On his return, he filled his chair once more, and continued to publish essays and poems; he also took some practical interest in politics, his indignation having been aroused by the scandals of Grant's second administration. In 1877 he was appointed minister to Spain, and in 1880 was advanced to the English mission, which he filled until 1885. No American has ever more worthily represented his country abroad, although it must be added that no very important diplomatic complications arose during his period of service. He was especially honoured in Great Britain, where he delivered some admirable memorial addresses on great writers, as well as a most thoughtful discourse on *Democracy* (Birmingham, October 6, 1884), which represents him at his highest as a patriotic publicist. He returned shortly after to America, saddened by the death of his second wife. During the years that elapsed before his own death on August 12, 1891, he superintended a revised edition of his writings, wrote a few articles and poems, and delivered addresses, that on *The Place of the Independent in Politics* being noteworthy. He had become more than a great man of letters of whose international fame his countrymen were proud; for in the eyes of many he was the greatest force for civic enlightenment and inspiration in a period when political reform was sorely needed.

As one looks back upon Lowell's career and examines his works, which have been increased by the publication of many posthumous volumes, notably by his excellent correspondence, one is inclined to regard him as having possessed the most full, varied, and ripened genius of any American man of letters; yet one must acknowledge that in creative literature proper his achievement was not commensurate with his genius. He was an eminent rather than a great poet, and one wonders whether this is not true of his criticism as well. As a brilliant, stimulating, highly individual essayist, who dealt in large measure with literary topics, his place is supreme in American literature and high in the literature written in English. He must also be ranked as a brilliant letter-writer and as a publicist of lofty ideals and important accomplishment. But whether he has made

or is making either an intense appeal to a
limited class of readers or a strong, broad
appeal to a large public is a question the answer to which is not easy to give. His high
place in the history of American literature is
however, secure, and he seems sure of a
select public happily situated between the
mass of readers and the exponents of ultra-
sophistication.

Along with the four New England poets
just treated and with Bryant, Emerson, and
Poe, a number of minor but not uninteresting
poets were writing in America during the
generation that preceded the war between
the States. One of these, Nathaniel Parker
Willis, has been already mentioned. Most of
his poems have been forgotten save the
pathetic lyric entitled *Unseen Spirits*. His
fiction and his gossiping book of European
experiences *Pencillings by the Way* are as
dead as his poetry, and the details of his
once conspicuous career as a journalist are
almost forgotten save when he comes in
contact with Poe. Yet there are many more
famous careers that are less instructive than
his and his gossip will still repay readers
interested in the literature and society of
three generations ago.

Besides Willis one may also recall a
writer already treated in another connection,
the Southern romancer, William Gilmore

Simms, who wrote several volumes of poetry from which a few lyrics have found their way into anthologies. Another poet, who links the North and South, is Albert Pike, author of *Dixie*, an interesting example of the writer of too precocious talents whose energies are dissipated along the numerous lines of activity a democracy offers to any young man of unusual capacity. Pike was one of the earliest of American poets to fall under the influence of Keats, and in his early *Hymns to the Gods* he displayed a promise that aroused expectations destined to remain unfulfilled. In almost complete contrast to Pike who, though New England born, became a frontier lawyer and a Confederate general, stands Dr. Thomas William Parsons of Boston, author of an incomplete translation of " The Divine Comedy," often praised, and of some impressive *Lines on a Bust of Dante.* Interesting though many of these minor poets are, especially some of the Transcendentalists, they are, after all, of but slight consequence to any class of readers except for an occasional poem which patriotic and never too exclusive anthologists are sure to have gathered.

CHAPTER VIII

THE HISTORIANS

THE writing of history in America, from the very nature of the colonial experiment, dates practically from the foundation of the earliest English plantations. First came narratives of contemporary events and descriptions of the New World, that is to say, a body of materials for history, and then in due time followed formal historical narratives. Many of the colonial historians, such as Governor Bradford of Plymouth, Governor Winthrop of Massachusetts Bay, and Robert Beverley of Virginia, are interesting both as men and as writers, and one, Governor Thomas Hutchinson of Massachusetts, has been highly praised for the scholarly qualities of his work. The Revolution and the formative period that followed it saw both the making and the writing of much history, one of the most important books of the period being Chief Justice John Marshall's *Life of Washington*. On the whole, however, the writing of history and the gathering of historical materials on a large scale and in a comparatively modern way may be said to have begun with Jared Sparks and with Washington Irving.

Sparks (1789-1866) was a Unitarian clergyman, a professor of history, and, later, president of Harvard. He was a pioneer searcher of archives and rendered great service by publishing the *Diplomatic Correspondence of the American Revolution* and the works of Washington and Franklin. He also contributed on a large scale to American biography, and his faults as an editor should not seriously diminish the gratitude of a later generation for his immense industry in gathering materials and in stimulating a patriotic interest in history. A more popular and important historian than Sparks was George Bancroft (1800-1891), still, probably, the best known of the writers who have devoted themselves specifically to the history of North America. He was a native of Massachusetts, a graduate of Harvard, and one of the first Americans to study in Germany. The initial volume of his elaborate *History of the United States* appeared in 1834, and won favour, largely through its full-flown rhetorical qualities, so suited to the public of the Jacksonian period. Two volumes followed after moderate intervals, and then the historian was somewhat submerged in the politician, for Bancroft served as Secretary of the Navy and as Minister to England. The latter post afforded him facilities for gathering materials, and on his return to America he resumed the publication of his history. Later he served as Minister to Prussia and to the German Empire, and the year 1874, which saw his retirement from his last diplomatic post, saw also the publication of his tenth volume, which carried the story only through the Revolution. In the forty years he had not ceased to be the rhetorician and philosopher of his earlier volumes, but he had become in addition a painstaking, minute historian of the modern type. In 1882 he completed his work by two volumes covering the formation of the Constitution and then, at a period when most men would have thought only of rest, he began to revise and compress his truly monumental history. Both in the fuller and in the reduced form of six volumes the work is of great importance to students, and its author should be regarded as a patriotic public servant and a historical student of immense industry and marked ability ; but he was not a great writer, and, although he will continue to be much more famous than rivals like the accurate and. partisan Richard Hildreth, or historians with more limited fields, such as Judge Gayarré, the scholarly historian of Louisiana, he is not likely to be read *in extenso* either for pleasure or for edification by persons whose reading is not done to order.

This means that Bancroft was not a true man of letters, an attractive writer like the late John Fiske, who, after he turned from philosophy, made the history of America from its discovery to the beginnings of federal government interesting to thousands of readers. And even on the side of research Bancroft has been followed by specialists in colonial history who have made good use of their advantages of increased materials and improved methods. The history of the republic since the adoption of the Constitution has also been treated in elaborate works covering larger and smaller periods. Some of these historians, for example, Henry Adams, James Schouler, John Bach McMaster, and James Ford Rhodes, have won deservedly high reputations; and the development of the spirit of historical research throughout the country by means of active historical societies and strong university departments of history, as well as various instrumentalities for the preservation of archives, state and national, has been noteworthy since the Civil War. On the whole, however, the American historians who have dealt with the history of their own country, with the exception of Parkman, have tended to be more eminent as exponents of the scientific study and presentation of history than as exponents of the art of historical narration.

By common consent the three greatest American masters of the art of historical narration are three natives of Massachusetts,— Prescott, Motley, and Parkman. That they and many other American historians should have done their work near the libraries of Cambridge and Boston is no cause for surprise, when one remembers that New England during their prime was the centre of American literature, and that it was the most favoured region of the country with respect to accumulated wealth and culture. It may be remarked, however, that perhaps the most famous of the American scholars who have done their work in the field of European history, Henry Charles Lea, was a citizen of a city that vies with Boston as a seat of wealth and long-established culture— Philadelphia.

The first of the important successors of Irving in the writing of elaborate works dealing with large European themes, particularly such themes as bore upon the early history of the new world, was William Hickling Prescott (1796-1859), the historian of the reign of Ferdinand and Isabella and of the conquests of Mexico and Peru. He was a native of Salem and a graduate of Harvard, who suffered in early manhood an accident which nearly deprived him of sight. This did not quench the ambition of emulating Gibbon

as a historian on a grand scale. He was
fortunately able to secure books and amanu-
enses, and to accumulate and arrange great
masses of notes, which he converted into
narratives well ordered and couched in a
dignified and attractive style. The difficulties
under which he laboured were immense ; but
his indomitable will, his high ambitions, and
his exceptional endowments as a scholar and
writer enabled him to win for himself an
international reputation, which, although it
has suffered through causes no one could
have foreseen, is still enviable. His attempts
in the field of biography and literary criticism
prove him to have been a man of letters in
the true sense of the phrase, but they do
little to-day to preserve his memory. He lives
as one of the most readable of descriptive
historians.

His first historical work of consequence
was the three volumes devoted to the period
of Ferdinand and Isabella, which appeared in
1837. It was so favourably received that
Prescott was encouraged to essay another
theme, one even more picturesque as well as
more definitely and extensively connected
with America. Six years later, in 1843, the
new work, the *History of the Conquest of
Mexico*, brought Prescott to the zenith of his
fame. It is his best book as a brilliant historical narrative, but it has suffered greatly

as a source of reliable information owing to
the fact that he was forced to depend upon
sources coloured by the imagination of the
Spanish conquerors and at variance with
conceptions of the state of Mexican development formed by modern archæologists and
anthropologists as the result of their researches.
Four years later came the companion work,
the almost equally interesting *History of the
Conquest of Peru*. Then Prescott girded
himself to a still greater task, his *History of
the Reign of Philip II.*, which was left un-
finished, only three volumes having appeared
during his life.

Apart from the fact that more than any of his
rivals Prescott has suffered from the invali-
dating of his materials and his views, it may
be doubted whether he was as great as a
historian in two very important respects,—
in his insight into character, and in his
interest in institutions and politics. In his
ideals of scholarly accuracy and in his energy
and courage he need fear no comparisons, nor
has any other American historian been more
gifted with a sense for the picturesque and
epic elements in history. It cannot be proved
that he was a better artist than Motley or
Parkman—indeed partisans of the last named
would probably smile at the suggestion that
such a view could be held. Yet it might be
contended by some readers with a taste for

classical balance and perfection of form and
style that Prescott combines dignity, ease,
interest, and a sense of proportion more
completely than almost any other writer of
his class. If he had been as fortunate as a
scholar as he was successful as an artist, he
would seem to many to be the greatest of
American historians. As it is, he is well
worthy to rank among great modern writers
of prose.

John Lothrop Motley, the historian of the
Dutch Republic, was born in 1814 in Dorchester, Massachusetts, now a part of the
city of Boston, and died near Dorchester,
England, in 1877. He was well connected,
his circumstances favoured his adopting the
life of a scholar and writer to which his tastes
inclined him, and he received the best
education America and Europe could afford.
He attended a school of which the historian
Bancroft was joint-principal, he graduated
from Harvard, and then he heard lectures at
Berlin and Göttingen, becoming the warm
personal friend of the man afterwards famous
as Prince Bismarck. He was handsome and a
social favourite, but, despite all other allure-
ments, he remained true to his love of books
and his literary ambitions. After an early
marriage to a sister of the poet Park Benjamin,
he tried his hand at a story, *Morton's Hope*,
which proved unsuccessful. Another work of

M

fiction, the colonial romance, *Merry Mount*, was kept in manuscript until 1849, when it, too, failed on publication. Meanwhile the rebuffed but not disheartened author had had his first experience of diplomatic life as secretary for a short time of the legation at St. Petersburg, had dabbled in Massachusetts politics, and had done some writing for the *North American Review*. He had also become interested in Dutch history, and with Prescott's approval he chose an episode of that reign of Philip II. which occupied the last years of the older historian. Finding materials difficult to obtain in America he sailed for Europe in 1851.

Five years later he issued at his own expense in London—for Murray refused the work—his *Rise of the Dutch Republic*, the success of which was extraordinary both with scholars and with the public. Then he took up the narrative at 1584, and in 1860 published the first two volumes of his *History of the United Netherlands*, much of the study for which had been done at the Hague, where he was cordially assisted by Dutch scholars. He was not so absorbed, however, in the early history of an alien people as to be oblivious to the great events taking place in his own country. He wrote letters to the *Times* which helped to influence English opinion in favour of the Union, he returned to America for a short period, and he accepted and filled until 1867 the mission to Austria, thus ranking himself with Irving, Bancroft, and others among our historian-diplomatists. After resigning his post he went to London, and in 1869 published the two remaining volumes of the *United Netherlands*, which carry the narrative to 1609. Then after a short visit to the country from which he had become practically an honoured exile, he returned to London as Minister to England, only to be suddenly recalled the next year in a way which aroused resentment in his friends. Study and travel brought consolation, however, and in 1874 he issued *The Life and Death of John Barneveld*. Three years later he died in England, where his daughters lived, and where he himself was more at home than in America.

Motley the man is interesting, and his letters, which were edited by his friend George William Curtis (1824-1892), himself one of the best essayists and publicists America has produced, are thoroughly entertaining, although perhaps making a greater appeal to English readers than to American. But it is almost entirely as a historian that he impresses posterity and that he holds his place in American literature. As compared with Prescott he is more fortunate in that his materials have worn better, and he will seem to many readers to be more brilliant and more inspiring through his manifest love of liberty; yet it may well be questioned whether he is on the whole so consummate an artist in the construction of his books as was the elder historian. As compared with Parkman, he has not the advantage of a theme touching so directly the fortunes of America, and in some respects he does not bear so well the scrutiny of minute scholars; yet he has the advantages that flow from a compact, dramatic, and inspiring theme, he seldom seems monotonous, he often rises to genuine eloquence. He is an extraordinarily skilful painter of portraits; whether or not he was always true to nature, he was always impressive in his drawing and in his use of the most effective colours. Perhaps he was not altogether a great stylist, or at least an impeccable one, but his writing so answered the varying needs of his narrative, as well as his own intellectual and spiritual moods, that it seems supererogatory to question his high place as a writer of prose. Perhaps his chief fault as a historian is the chief fault of that school of Macaulay and Michelet to which he belonged, the fault of partisanship springing from an excess of emotions commendable when held in check. Motley was not by temperament or training very well qualified to be impartial toward Calvinists or Spaniards.

He was specially qualified to celebrate with stirring eloquence the heroic achievements of a people and a leader inspired with his own overmastering passion, the love of liberty. Eloquence, liberal aspirations, command of the bolder and larger elements of the art of historical narration—these are the salient features of Motley the historian. Brilliant descriptive powers, a keen sense for social and political life, and cosmopolitan experience —these are what we chiefly remember when we think of Motley the diplomatist and correspondent. His books have become classics in their kind ; and it is scarcely profitable to ask whether, on the whole, they are superior or inferior to the works of the two American historians with whom one naturally compares him.

Francis Parkman, of Boston, who was born in 1823 and died seventy years later, was the youngest of our most distinguished group of historians, and hence the one most markedly affected by modern ideals of scholarship. Probably his minute, painstaking accuracy, which he managed to combine with an excellent style and exceptional powers of description and construction, has done much to prompt latter-day students and readers of history to give him the palm over his rivals. His subject, too, lying as it does to the north and west and not to the south of what is now the United States, seems, despite its close connection with the old world and with an un-English civilization, more completely American than the themes of Prescott and Motley, and gives Parkman a patriotic appeal. This patriotic appeal links him with the school of historians who have treated the history of the United States proper, and doubtless explains in part the attraction he exerts upon many readers ; for since the success of the Union cause in the Civil War a noticeable national self-consciousness has exhibited itself both in the spirit and substance of American books and in the tastes of American readers.

Parkman was a delicate boy and hence was kept much in the country, a fact which doubtless accounts in part for that love of nature and of life in the wild which he never lost and from which his books profited greatly. He was also enabled, before he graduated from Harvard, to travel in Europe, and after graduation he studied law but did not practise. In 1846 he set out from St. Louis to explore the then far west, the region of the Rockies. He lived for some months among Indian tribes, and learned much about them and about the ways of trappers. He embodied his experiences in magazine articles which in 1847 he made into his first book, *The Oregon Trail*. This remains a most readable and popular narrative of adventure and exploration, which gives information to mature students with regard to the west as it was on the point of passing from the control of the savage to that of civilized man. It is also read in schools as an English prose classic ; and it deserves the honour on account of its attractive style, its powers of description and straightforward narration, its sympathy with nature and uncramped men, and its historical importance. It was an extraordinarily good first book, and foreshadowed its author's subsequent success as a picturesque historian who, nevertheless, was careful of his facts.

Parkman's health was much injured by exposure during his sojourn in the west, and he never recovered. He was no more daunted, however, than Prescott had been, and the annals of literature contain little or nothing more heroic than his devotion to his great task. For some years he could not work at all, and often during his working periods he could read or write only for a few minutes together. He was sufficiently well off to have a large amount of copying of documents done for him, and to secure the reading of these and of all necessary books on his chosen theme—the struggle of France and Great Britain for the control of the major portion of North America. He was also able to make extensive journeys both for the personal consultation of archives and for the acquisition of topographical information. He studied nature, too, and he made the most of the early experiences that had so hampered him by undermining his health. The result was a series of eleven volumes dealing with a subject which, as we have seen, was as important to the understanding of the development of America, as it was attractive to lovers of old-world romance and of new-world freshness and untrammelled freedom. The actors in the drama Parkman had to unfold called for the resources of both a bold and a subtle portrait-painter, and the historian answered the demand, falling, perhaps, not a whit below Motley in this important point. Scene after scene of thrilling interest had to be painted vividly, yet with minute fidelity, and here again Parkman met all the requirements of his theme. It is no wonder that with his faithfulness, his thoroughness, his brilliant artistic powers, he should have made, as we have said, a deeper appeal to modern readers than any other American historian. He seems to have no discomfiture to fear at the hands of archæologists ; he has no disastrous comparisons to fear, since he rules alone in a spacious and unique realm of his own. One thinks of Parkman when one thinks of Montcalm and Wolfe, of Jesuit missionaries and

coureurs de bois threading the wilds, of forest
fighting, of voyages of discovery on mighty
streams—and one's critical faculties are, at
least for the time being, held in abeyance.

Parkman's historical series began in 1851
with the two volumes, *The Conspiracy of
Pontiac*, which treated the Indian uprising of
1763. Then followed, after a long interval,
Pioneers of France in the New World, which
appeared in 1865. *The Jesuits in North
America* and *La Salle and the Discovery of the
Great West* came next at intervals of two
years. Five years later, 1874, appeared *The
Old Régime in Canada*, and three years afterwards *Count Frontenac and New France under
Louis XIV*. *A Half Century* was the last
volume to be published in point of time,
its date being 1892, the year before its author's
death ; but the true conclusion of the series
is to be found in the two volumes of 1884
entitled *Montcalm and Wolfe*, in which,
according to some, Parkman's genius as a
historian appears in its fullest splendour. *The
Old Régime in Canada* may appeal more to
certain readers; but, after all, it is idle to
make such comparisons, except for the purpose of bringing out the growth of Parkman's
powers. These are visible, indeed, in *The
Conspiracy of Pontiac*, the first instalment of
the series, but they increased greatly with
years and experience, whether we consider the

flexible style, or examine the skill with which character is analyzed or complex materials ordered. The entire group of volumes constitutes a life work of which any historian since Gibbon might be proud; when Parkman's physical disabilities are duly weighed, one is at a loss to name a more creditable or more truly wonderful achievement in the annals of literature, the supremely creative masters excepted. Some reservations some readers will doubtless make. The scale may seem too large for what is after all an episode, and when read in succession the instalments of the story may seem monotonous. But when all deductions have been made, Parkman and his books will remain objects of scarcely alloyed admiration.

Like Motley, Froude, and other historians, Parkman tried his hand at fiction. His single novel, *Vassall Morton* (1856), was an impossible medley, and one prefers to consider that Parkman showed his versatility better as a professor of horticulture at Harvard and a writer on roses than as a novelist or romancer. Perhaps if he had been instead a professor of history, he would still have made his histories fascinating; yet one is not sure, since Germanized professors seem to pay slight attention to style, and one is glad to have him just as he was, a somewhat solitary and secluded figure concentrated upon a great task.

We must not be unjust, however, to professors, especially to the distinguished occupants of one great chair at Harvard. The predecessor of Longfellow and Lowell, the scholarly George Ticknor (1791-1871), may well be grouped with the historians, both because he was Prescott's biographer and because his *History of Spanish Literature* was an exhaustive treatise on the literature of the country which had so fascinated Irving and Prescott. Ticknor, too, with Edward Everett, set an example to Bancroft and Motley by going to Germany to study; and in his exact scholarship he was a model and an inspiration to most of the men we have treated in this chapter. He is more interesting to the general reader through his valuable and entertaining *Life, Letters, and Journals* of 1876 than he is through his still authoritative treatise on Spanish literature; but, perhaps, his greatest service was rendered as a pioneer of modern scholarship in the new world.

CHAPTER IX

WEBSTER AND LINCOLN

IT is said, perhaps not with entire justice, that the art of oratory is dying in America. It is certainly nearer the truth to say that many good orators have died in America within the past century and a half, and that most of their works have died with them. It is the good fortune of Patrick Henry that his fame is maintained almost entirely by tradition. Other early orators, including preachers, are remembered by name, but their names mean little save to the special student. Even the once famous Edward Everett of Massachusetts, scholar, Governor, Minister to England, president of Harvard, United States Senator, Secretary of State, and orator and lecturer upon innumerable subjects on innumerable occasions is now unread, although accessible in massive volumes and a model of latter-day classic eloquence if ever there was one. The less academic but perhaps even more " golden tongued " orator-statesman of Kentucky, Henry Clay, probably the most intensely idolized of American political leaders, is almost unreadable; while his fervent admirer, Abraham Lincoln who did not anticipate literary renown, is more read than many distinguished professional writers of a generation ago, and holds a good place among American authors. Clay's great contemporary, John C. Calhoun of South Carolina, is still read by students, not so much for his literary merits, as because he is the most eminent expositor of the doctrine of Staterights and the most acute analyst and defender of the constitutional rights of minorities. Robert Y. Hayne of South Carolina is still read and remembered as Webster's far from feeble opponent in the greatest forensic contest in American history; but most of the orators contemporary with him have become mere names save to the student of politics. Even the greatest of anti-slavery orators, the passionate advocate of freedom, Wendell Phillips, is probably read less and less as the years go by, although his genius as a speaker was indisputable and his moral courage worthy of the highest praise. It is true that Phillips was a fanatic, but his comparative eclipse, from the point of view of literary fame, is not due to that fact. His fate is but another illustration of the truth that the spoken word when set down in writing becomes literature only in very rare cases.

Have the works of the greatest of American orators, Daniel Webster, become literature ? Editors of his works and of selections of them for use in schools, biographers, historians, critics have vied with one another in assuring us that his position as a man of letters is secure. He has been ranked—by Americans —with Demosthenes and Cicero, and some perfervid patriots seem to prefer him to both of those great orators. They appear to regard the *Reply to Hayne* as the greatest speech ever delivered. That he is the greatest of American orators, that his rank as a statesman is very high, that his services as a patriot to the cause of union can scarcely be over-estimated, that his speeches as literature deserve grateful and admiring perusal— these are claims in his behalf that should win cordial assent. But that Webster was the superior of Cicero or Burke as a writer is a statement that can be made with impunity only in the bosom of one's parish. But then America is a very large parish.

Webster was born in New Hampshire in 1782, and early astonished his rural neighbours by his oratorical gifts. He soon became the best lawyer in his State, and in his thirty-first year he entered Congress, where he distinguished himself. In 1816 he removed to Boston, his later fame being thus associated with Massachusetts, although as a matter of fact he was the chief political and legal glory of New England at large, and for many years the idol of the Whig party throughout the Union. In 1817 he resigned from Congress, and devoted himself for some time to his great practice, winning in this year one of his most famous victories in behalf of his *alma mater*, Dartmouth College. He was now the foremost advocate in the country, and one of the greatest interpreters of the constitution. As a commemorative orator he was also without a rival from 1820, when he delivered his oration on the two hundredth anniversary of the landing of the Puritans, which was followed in a few years by orations on the laying of the corner stone of the Bunker Hill Monument and on the almost simultaneous deaths of John Adams and Thomas Jefferson. These utterances were not only inspiring to American patriots, but full of educational value to the not very sophisticated generation that heard them. They have not lost this value, although one may doubt their importance in the literature of the world.

In 1822, before the two orations mentioned last were delivered, Webster returned to Congress; and five years later he was sent to represent Massachusetts in the Senate, where he advocated protection and defended the theory of an indissoluble Union. Here, in 1830, he delivered that *Reply to Hayne* in which he is seen at his highest as orator, patriot, and statesman. He is too large to be described in any one phrase, but we do him no great injustice when we say that his highest claim to remembrance lies in the fact that during a most critical period of our history he was beyond all other men the spokesman of the Union. The country Washington had founded and Jefferson had expanded was stirred by the voice of Webster to a consciousness of its life and aims that enabled Lincoln and Grant to save it from dismemberment. The *Reply to Hayne* is less important as a contribution to constitutional history than some of its admirers have deemed, but it and other of Webster's deliverances in the Senate, where with Calhoun and Clay he made up a great triumvirate, deserve the amplest praise as expressions of national ideals.

The remainder of his career, which was closed in 1852, requires but few words. He retained his fame as a great advocate, he was constantly lured on by the hope that he might reach the presidency, he rendered excellent services as Secretary of State, then alas! he disappointed the hopes of the anti-slavery men by his support of Clay's Compromise of 1850. Whittier's terrible denunciation in *Ichabod* did him injustice, for Webster was too completely a child of the age of compromises to be able to see, as Lincoln did, that the cause of the Union and the cause of human freedom were one and inseparable. His famous *Seventh of March Speech*, which alienated so many admirers, was a more mistaken but no less sincere effort to preserve the Union than the *Reply to Hayne*. It prevents one, however, from claiming for Webster the highest tribute that can be given to a public man, the tribute that is due to clearsighted and bold defence, against all odds, of the cause of truth and freedom. Unfortunately, also, Webster must be denied high encomiums upon his private life. The temptations to which he succumbed were great, especially during his generation, and he was encouraged to yield to them by the foolish shortsightedness of his admirers, who perhaps deserve more blame than he does. But, when all deductions are made, he remains a notable and a noble figure, almost gigantic in his powers, though certainly not in literature the demi-god he once seemed to be.

It has become the fashion of late to treat Abraham Lincoln as more than a demi-god; and yet, singularly enough, a growing realization of the breadth and depth of his humane qualities is responsible in large measure for the apotheosizing process that has been going on ever since, at the zenith of his noble

N

career, he fell a victim to the folly and fury of a fanatic assassin. To describe his life here would be as superfluous as a similar attempt would have been in the case of the American with whom one naturally associates him, Benjamin Franklin. Both were self-educated; both rose to fame and eminence rather through the possession of what we call character than through the exhibition of those saliently brilliant and rare features of mind and spirit which are usually associated with genius; both used literature as a means to an end, not as an art worthy of their entire devotion; both owe it in considerable measure to their writings that they live to-day in the hearts of their countrymen in a more vital fashion than if they depended for fame solely upon what biographers and historians have written about them. Franklin, through his versatility displayed as man of business, citizen, diplomatist, statesman, scientist, philanthropist, humorist, and general man of letters and affairs, seems to be the more wonderful personality; Lincoln, through the tremendous importance of the services he rendered America and mankind and through the simple loftiness of his character, impresses one as the greater man, the nobler soul. Both derive much from contact with the soil, from racy, homely qualities; neither belongs with men like Milton and Washington and Robert

E. Lee, whose genius is essentially aristocratic. Both make a naturally strong appeal to a democracy, which, through a quite justifiable pride in such of its great men as do not stand aloof, is just as naturally inclined slightly to exaggerate their merits and to overlook their defects.

Lincoln's superiority over Franklin as a man accounts for such superiority over his great predecessor as he shows as a writer. The severely simple eloquence of the Gettysburg Address would probably not have been possible to Franklin, despite the fact that he too had access to the Bible and Shakespeare for inspiration. The tastes of his time would have been against him, as well as his own comparative lack of the spiritual and the poetic. Lincoln thought just as much of the people as Franklin, nevertheless at times he drew apart from them and dwelt in spiritual solitude, thus partaking in a measure with the great lonely geniuses of the race. Hence comes the high seriousness of his writings when he is at his best, in the two inaugurals, in the speech at Cooper Union in 1860, in some of his letters. In variety of semi-creative power, as essayist, humorist, and narrator Franklin displays a wider range of genius, and in some respects is nearer to an accomplished, though not deliberate, man of letters than is Lincoln. But in quality of inspiration he seems to be greatly Lincoln's inferior. One prefers to associate the great President rather with that noble ethical stimulator, Emerson. Perhaps more than any other Americans since Washington these two have made noble ideals of life, public and private, seem realizable to their countrymen. In their writings sounds more clearly than anywhere else, perhaps, that " citizen note " which seems, as we have said, to be the most distinctive quality of American literature. Lincoln shares also with Longfellow the power of simple straightforward appeal to the unsophisticated heart. Hence, given his great place in history, it is no wonder that his place in American literature should be with the greatest and the most truly national of all our writers, that his speeches should be read while those of Everett and Clay are forgotten, that he should long since have surpassed even the mighty Webster in attracting to himself the admiration and appreciation of the entire American people. His successor is not in sight, not only because no crisis has arisen in which it has been possible, for any man to render public services commensurate with his, but because no American has since been able to use the vernacular at once so simply and so nobly.

CHAPTER X

HARRIET BEECHER STOWE

MRS. STOWE illustrates conspicuously those traits of the Puritan temper which in Hawthorne were obscure. Like others of the Beecher family, she had the gift of making her dreams tell in real life. If we are to judge by the passion it stirred and the reform it heralded, she wrote the most effective novel in American literature; but apart from her imaginative writing she exerted powerfully all the influences of a good citizen. Her scorn of evil was as practical as her praise of righteousness. All her service was touched with chivalrous errantry.

The very effectiveness of her genius has placed her literary fame in some jeopardy. Her great book was so closely implicated with the cause it served that the world lets it recede into an historic past with the other documents of the great war; and measured by this almost military efficiency her other books seem, even as historical documents, comparatively negligible; so that all her writing, in one way or the other, seems likely to be underestimated. But no one would have cared less than herself, since her work was accomplished and her spirit remains.

Harriet Elizabeth Beecher was born on June 14, 1811, at Litchfield, Connecticut, where her father, the Rev. Dr. Lyman Beecher, was pastor. From her mother, Roxana Foote, as well as from her father, Harriet inherited great energy and religious fervour. After her mother's death, in 1815, she was for a time with her grandmother, at Guilford, Connecticut ; in 1817 her father married Miss Harriet Porter, who proved an excellent stepmother. But the chief influence of Harriet's youth was her elder sister, Catherine, who had started a school in Hartford. When Dr. Beecher in 1826 became pastor of the Hanover Street Church in Boston, Harriet stayed with her sister.

In 1832, however, the entire family removed to Walnut Hills, near Cincinnati, where Dr. Beecher had accepted the Presidency of the Lane Theological Seminary. It was at Walnut Hills that Harriet discovered her gift, with a prize short story in a local magazine. It was there that she met and married, January 6, 1836, Professor Calvin E. Stowe, who taught in the seminary. From Walnut Hills three years earlier she had made a visit to Kentucky, where she had seen the institution of slavery in its happier aspects. It was from her home, in 1839, that Professor Stowe and Henry Ward Beecher saved a free coloured girl who was being pursued by her former master. In Cincinnati near by, the pro-slavery mobs burned the printing houses where emancipation had been advocated, and one editor, J. P. Lovejoy, was murdered. Lovejoy was a friend of the Beechers. It was at Walnut Hills, then, that Mrs. Stowe lived the experiences which she converted into her book.

Her early sketches were published in 1843, under the title of *The Mayflower*. In 1849 Dr. Stowe became a professor in Bowdoin College, and his family removed to Brunswick, Maine, in April, 1850. A month before, New England's indignation had been roused by Webster's defence of Henry Clay's compromise; and the passage of the Fugitive Slave Act, by which citizens in free States were required to assist in the recovery of slave " property," convinced Mrs. Stowe, as well as many other Northerners, that the time for action was at hand. In February, 1851, she began writing *Uncle Tom's Cabin*, the first instalment of which appeared in the *National Era*, June 5. In book form it was published in Boston, March 20, 1852, and its enormous and continuous sale began at once.

Mrs. Stowe's life from that time was eventful and full of accomplishment, but the significance of it had been conditioned by her previous experiences. She had inherited missionary fervour, and had seen what it is to be oppressed, and she devoted herself naturally to any cause of enfranchisement that presented itself. Of the outward details of her career it need only be recorded that she was twice abroad ; and on her first trip just after the publication of *Uncle Tom's Cabin*, she was welcomed with remarkable honour in England and Scotland. In 1852 her husband became professor in the Andover Theological Seminary, and in 1863 the family removed from Andover to Hartford, which was their final home. After the war Mrs. Stowe bought a place at Mandarin, Florida, and interested herself practically in the South. Her chief publications, after *Uncle Tom's Cabin*, were *Dred*, 1856, *The Minister's Wooing*, 1858, *The Pearl of Orr's Island*, 1862, *Agnes of Sorrento*, 1863, *Old Town Folks*, 1869, *Old Town Fireside Stories*, 1871, *My Wife and I*, 1872, *We and Our Neighbours*, 1875, *Poganuc People*, 1878. Mrs. Stowe died at Hartford, July 1, 1876, and was buried at Andover.

Her novels are of two quite different kinds. Her reputation was made by a novel with a purpose, and she followed her theme in a second story ; her early writing, however, and most of her later books dealt with the New England of her girlhood. If this second kind of story is less thought of now when her name is mentioned, at least the literary historian knows that in this field she was a pioneer. It is her picture of New England, rather than Hawthorne's, which has been imitated; it is with her that the work of Miss Sarah Orne Jewett or Mrs. Mary Wilkins-Freeman is associated. She therefore has a double place in American literature, with a masterpiece in one field and pioneer triumphs in another.

In a certain sense *Uncle Tom's Cabin* was intended as propaganda; Mrs. Stowe believed that if slavery were once clearly seen, it would be abandoned. She therefore wished to represent the institution as it was. Since it was a national institution, the guilt of it was in her opinion national. She had no intention of seeming to pass judgment on the South. Indeed, the cruel slave-dealers and the fiendish plantation owner in the story are Northerners, and Miss Ophelia, who cannot understand the negroes and serves them only by way of self-sacrifice, is a New Englander. St. Clare, Eva's father, the attractive character of the book, is a Southerner, and the pleasantest home described is that of the Shelbys, in Kentucky. Mrs. Stowe had, as she thought, taken pains to show that slavery was as injurious to Northern individuals as to Southern, and she was surprised when the South thought her portraiture uncomplimentary.

Of literary art in any superficial sense, *Uncle Tom's Cabin* has very little. It has the extreme simplicity of great art, however; and it imparts that confidence that the reader is seeing the truth which only a great book can impart. Carlyle wrote to its author that he knew the story represented the facts truthfully, although he had never seen the life it recorded. This self-evident veracity gave the novel its power; against counter-charges and contradictions innumerable, its testimony was unshaken. And beyond the immediate cause which it served, it has become the one widely known record of the South before the war, as Cooper's novels, rightly or wrongly, have become the world record of the American Indian, and as Bret Harte's stories have become the world memory of the California miners.

In her Western experiences Mrs. Stowe had seen some of slavery's demoralizing effects, upon both the slave and the owner. In this book, however, she was chiefly concerned with the slave. She struck at the cardinal defect of slavery—the fact that it was not, as its defenders claimed, a patriarchal institution, nor could it be so long as slaves, like other property, were subject to sale. The Southern apologists held that the masters were in general humane, and provided for the negro better than he could provide for himself; and such masters, and such fortunate slaves, Mrs. Stowe had seen on her Kentucky visit. But she had had other experience of what often happened when the kind master died, and the slaves passed to less kind, even cruel, hands, and the members of one family were scattered, perhaps never to see each other again. Worse than that, even during the life of a kind master, a valuable slave might be seized for debt, and the more valuable the slave, the more surely the creditors would seize him.

The novel, then, is a study of this separation of slaves by sale. Though the picture of Southern life is filled in with details, the emphasis is upon those critical moments when the " property " is dispersed. Uncle Tom, who has made himself valuable by efforts to be truly religious and civilized, is sold for his master's debts. Mr. Shelby, his master, parts with him reluctantly, and is pleased when the slave-dealer reports that Tom is sold into a good family. The sale proves, therefore, as slightly tragic as possible; nothing worse has happened than that Tom is separated from his wife and children. But Tom's second master, St. Clare, dies unexpectedly, and his selfish widow sells Tom, since he is one of the most valuable assets of the estate, and

he falls into the hands of a monster. Whether
or not the picture of Legree is overdrawn—
and Mrs. Stowe was convinced that he was not
so exceptional as her Southern critics claimed
—at least she had proved her indictment
against slavery; no system was patriarchal
in which the slave was transferred unexpectedly from master to master, although his
kinder masters had intended to set him free.
That Tom had served Mr. Shelby faithfully
was no protection when the mortgage-holding
slave-dealer set eyes upon him. Though he
eased Eva's life and became her beloved
comrade, and thereby earned the gratitude
of her father, it availed him nothing when
that father died. The episode of little Eva's
death, which appealed to the same phase of
mawkish sentiment that delighted in the
end of little Nell, has its real effect even now,
when it no longer produces tears; it shows
how near a slave like Tom could come to
human fellowship with the master, and yet
be sold. When St. Clare dies, the only
difference between Tom and the good-for-
nothing valet is that Tom's virtues give him
a higher market value. There could be
nothing patriarchal in a system which produced such a situation.

Yet it must be remembered that Mrs.
Stowe was not blind to the peculiarities of the
negro temperament. She had no quarrel

with those who said that the negro lent himself naturally to the institution of slavery.
That such a nature as Tom's needed protection, she never denied; but slavery, as it
operated upon Uncle Tom, was the very reverse of protection. She ascribes to Tom's
honesty the fact that he never ran away, and
she would not discredit her own testimony;
yet she is not unwilling we should observe
that it is the full-blooded negro who makes
no effort for his freedom. George Harris and
Eliza, whose lives are to be ruined by Mr.
Shelby's sale of their child, make a desperate
and successful attempt to be free. They,
however, are mulattoes. Their story is
secondary in the novel to the fate of
Uncle Tom, but secondary only because
they have the enterprise of their white
ancestors, and are therefore not typical
slaves.

In her next novel, *Dred*, Mrs. Stowe continued her pictures of the bad effects of slavery, but she now showed the influence of the
institution upon the white people rather than
upon their servants. By that very change of
purpose she gained in subtlety; to exhibit
the physical sufferings of Uncle Tom, or the
desperate peril of Eliza and George Harris,
required less fineness of imagination and led
to a less discriminating result, than to demonstrate the reaction of evil power upon him

who uses it. The novel was therefore considered by many competent readers an advance upon *Uncle Tom's Cabin*. If in the end it attained no such fame, the explanation is easily provided in that very subtlety of purpose and effect. It is less simple, less passionate, less coherent than the earlier book, but in many respects it is the richest of Mrs. Stowe's writings ; it contains most of that interpretation of life which we expect of a book whose intention is ethical.

Nina Gordon, the heroine, is mistress of a large plantation. She has one near relative, her brother Tom. She depends for advice in most matters, however, upon Harry, her slave overseer. Harry is her own half-brother, and knows that he is, but she is completely ignorant of her father's sin. Mrs. Stowe takes great pains to trace the steps by which the elder Gordon had convinced himself that his illegitimate son should not be acknowledged, nor set free, but should remain in the family to look after his white sister and brother. Unpleasant to Harry as the relation is, he finds it bearable until Tom returns—the incarnation of all the moral danger of slave-holding. Tom has become insolent and vicious, and instinctively feels something to resent in Harry's character. He falls in love with Harry's wife, and announces his purpose to buy her. That such a situation was possible, even frequent, in a slave-holding society Mrs. Stowe thought she had good proof. But even without proof, nothing in *Uncle Tom's Cabin* was so appalling an indictment of slavery as this possibility.

It is the fault of the book, however, that Mrs. Stowe is embarrassed by the wealth of her material. She proposes to herself so many problems that she has not time to solve them all reasonably. It seems unreasonable that Harry should save his wife so easily, if the peril was indeed so grave. And with the solution, or discarding, of this problem, Mrs. Stowe begins what is practically a new story, in the account of Clayton, a high-minded reformer, to whom Nina is engaged. Clayton illustrates the occasional effect of slavery upon the far-sighted white man, upon the individual who realized that only an improvement of conditions would save the country from terrible catastrophe. He therefore institutes reforms upon his plantation, teaching his negroes to read and write, and making himself the champion of the slaves, against the wish of his friends and relatives. In one of the best situations of the story he wins an unpopular case in court, only to have the decision reversed, on appeal, by the judge, his own father. He persuades Nina also to try the experiment of education on her own servants. But his happiness ends with her sudden and unaccounted-for death. His reforms then bring him into such disrepute that he is forced to leave the State. The problem which he illustrates is, therefore, in a measure unsolved; to say that he failed is not to answer the question as to the value of the experiment, had he been allowed to complete it.

There remains but one other problem in the story, and that is represented in the negro who gives his name to the book. Dred, like Cassy in *Uncle Tom's Cabin*, supplies that illustration of the love of mystery and supernaturalism without which no study of African character would be complete. From our first acquaintance with him, when from the darkness his voice sounds its prophecy over the camp-meeting, we expect in him some unusual revelation of power. In his refuge in the swamp, he appeals equally to the imagination, a born leader and inspired saviour of his race. But the situation of which he was the centre proved as impossible of solution as the other two. He is disposed of quite illogically when the slave-hunter's bullet kills him.

The one thoroughly successful theme in the story is subordinate, and we suspect that its success is accidental. The old negro, Tipp, who devoted himself to bringing up in a manner befitting their birth the destitute white children of the house he served, is as satisfactory a record of slavery as its most ardent champions could desire. The very limitations of Tipp's character—the fact that he is less heroic and less serviceable than Uncle Tom, and less emotional than Cassey or Dred, justifies him the more as a faithful portrait.

Apart from these two books, the bulk of Mrs. Stowe's work was devoted to New England. She was a realist of the best kind, who described faithfully, not from scientific motives of accuracy, but from affectionate memory. Her first published story, *Uncle Lot*, which had won the prize in the Cincinnati magazine, was of this kind, a study of the quiet, idealistic New England life ; and this subject she returned to in *The Pearl of Orr's Island*, and the *Old Town* books, and *Poganuc People*, which was in a sort a memorial of her own girlhood. The chief illustration of this side of her work, however, is *The Minister's Wooing*, which Lowell thought the best of her stories.

Much of the interest of this novel, to Mrs. Stowe, was in the theme of the supposed shipwreck of an unconverted son. She had just lost her son Henry, a student at Dartmouth, who was drowned while bathing in the Connecticut ; and about his spiritual state she

o

had such misgivings as only her old-fashioned theology was capable of. Her sister Catherine had suffered similar mental agony years before, over the death of her betrothed, about whose salvation the orthodox could not be sure. Mrs. Stowe evidently intended her sincere and touching statement of this sorrow to be the central interest of the book.

But the modern reader turns rather to Dr. Hopkins, the minister, and his fine sacrifice. Perhaps only a New Englander or a Scotchman could understand Mrs. Scudder's extreme ambition to marry her daughter Mary to the rather elderly minister. When Mary's lover, James Marvyn, is supposed to be drowned, Mary has no defence against her mother's hopes, and promises herself to Dr. Hopkins,—and then her lover returns. For once Mrs. Stowe was proof against the maudlin sentiment of those decades, and did not solve the problem by killing the heroine. Dr. Hopkins sees the situation and releases Mary so that she can love her true mate. The minister's sacrifice is told with fine humour, with no exaggeration of sentiment to impair its nobility.

It is perhaps useless to regret that it is only the stories dealing with slavery—or we may say, *Uncle Tom's Cabin*—which preserve Mrs. Stowe's fame, but it is not useless to repeat that her influence is felt in those New England stories of the American past, which have since been the model for many studies of other parts of her own country—perhaps even of countries overseas.

CHAPTER XI

WALT WHITMAN

WALT WHITMAN has been one of the most debated of American poets. He has been challenged, not, like Poe, as to the depth or importance of his poetic quality, but as to whether he has any poetic quality at all. By way of contrast, he has been praised as the greatest of American poets. At present his fame is on the increase, and although many readers still prefer the older verse music to his rugged chants, and persist in asking for some winnowing of taste in the subjects of poetry, yet few now deny the power of his imagination and the truly democratic reach of his sympathies. Doubtless, in a few years a majority of American critics will be glad to allow his claim as the representative poet of his country.

This improvement in his position has been aided by world-wide changes of taste in other arts than poetry, and by corresponding changes in æsthetic theory, which cannot be gone into here. But perhaps these changes rest on the larger change in mankind's vision of society which has gradually been brought about by the theory of evolution. Even the untrained man, sharing in a kind of diffused science, now thinks of all life as having inherent importance and dignity. In this attitude of mind lies the democratic idea, and also the very essence of Whitman's poetic theory and practice.

He was born at West Hills, Long Island, on May 31, 1819. His father, Walter Whitman, whose name he inherited and abbreviated, removed to Brooklyn in 1824; and after some attendance at the public schools, Whitman got a place in a lawyer's office, then in a doctor's, and finally learned the printer's trade. His school education he supplemented by enthusiastic reading in the more imaginative kinds of literature; Scott and *The Arabian Nights* were early favourites, and later the Bible, Shakespeare, Ossian, the best translated versions of Homer, Aeschylus, Sophocles, the old German Nibelungen, the ancient Hindoo poems, and one or two other masterpieces, Dante's among them. In 1838 he tried school teaching in the country, but returned to his printing and drifted into newspaper work. From 1848-1849 he edited the Brooklyn *Daily Eagle.* 1849 saw him in New Orleans, on the staff of the *Daily Crescent,* but two years later he was again in Brooklyn.

Leaves of Grass, his first volume, was published in 1855. Throughout his life he re-issued this volume with alterations and additions. His next volume, *Drum Taps*, 1865, was founded on his actual experiences in the war. He volunteered as an army nurse, and served faithfully in the hospitals and camps. After the war he was rewarded with government clerkships, which he held until 1874, when he suffered a stroke of paralysis. The rest of his life was spent in Camden, New Jersey. His later volumes of prose and verse were *Passage to India*, 1870; *Democratic Vistas*, 1870; *Memoranda during the War*, 1875; *Specimen Days and Collect*, 1882; *November Boughs*, 1888; and *Goodbye, My Fancy*, 1891. He died at Camden, March 26, 1892.

The poetry of Whitman made vigorous attacks upon tradition in both its matter and its manner. The twofold peculiarity, however, is from a single cause. Whitman was the conscientious prophet of naturalness, and his hand was against all conventions. To think of him as an irresponsible charlatan is to come furthest from a true valuation, for he had the literary background as much as any poet, and he is by far the most thoughtful of American poets. That he violated the traditions of verse rhythm, and that he introduced into his poems subject matter usually considered not fit for conversation, to say nothing of poetry, are obvious and comparatively unimportant facts. To dwell upon them would not explain his great power over so many men.

If we consider his philosophy in some detail, these aspects of his poetic work will explain themselves. He was in some essential ways a disciple of Emerson. That is, he believed in the self-sufficiency of the individual, in the divine possibilities of every man, in a common human nature so pervasive that what any man feels or thinks or knows is a matter of concern to all other men. Like Emerson, he believed that in himself was the solution of all his own questions; the only difference between them was in their taste. Of this precious seasoning of wisdom Whitman had almost none. Where Emerson looked into his own heart and tactfully quoted himself under the disguise of "the poet Osman," Whitman came out frankly with the personal pronoun, at the risk of seeming a prodigious egoist. Philosophically, however, they were equally modest, and it is essentially Emerson we are listening to when Whitman sings,

> " I celebrate myself;
> And what I assume, you shall assume;
> For every atom belonging to me, as good belongs to you."

But if Whitman shares with Emerson the

belief in the self-sufficiency of the individual soul, he does not at all share Emerson's adoration of solitude. On the contrary, Whitman's love of social man is his chief passion. With all possible emphasis upon the dignity of the individual, he contemplates the ideal man always in comradeship with his fellows. This point of view, which made him the true spokesman of democracy, and helped him to foresee the essential problems of his own country, was due chiefly to his genuine love of mankind. Whatever reinforcement of his affections he got from political or scientific theory, he was a democrat in his heart before he was in his mind. All things touched by human life were to him necessarily touched with emotion, charged with overtones, the truest subject of poetry. All the labours and pastimes of men were to him suggestive of poetic feeling; much as he loved nature, he liked best scenes of traffic in cities, crowded thoroughfares, in which there was the most varied contact with energetic human nature. This catholic sympathy for man in a state of social busy-ness is the key to those least successful poems of his in which he made what seems a catalogue of human occupations, merely naming the stevedore singing, the riflemen shooting, the raft-tenders blowing their bugles, the Arab calling to prayer. What is poetry but the expression of emotion

by select words or images or rhythms charged
with that emotion ? He could not think of
images more profoundly emotional than these
pictures of man's activity, and he believed
that the more of such images the poem contained, the wider and stronger its appeal.
That his theory was sound enough is illustrated by those humble but popular lyrics
which in every language speak to the heart by
images of childhood—the old home, mother
and father, the old playground, the cradle,
and the hearth. If these family images grip
the imagination of the family, should not the
race images grip the imagination of the race ?
This was Whitman's theory. He was giving
other men credit for a sympathy as tireless
as his own.

But this sympathy, which was his natural
gift, was powerfully reinforced by modern
science. He saw all life unified in evolution,
as Emerson saw it reposing in one Over-Soul.
Therefore he denied any distinction of hon-
ourableness between higher and lower forms,
for all forms are in the eyes of science equally
transfigured by the significance of life. In a
sense the lower biological forms are more
honourable than the higher, since the loss of
them would curtail so much more of the evo-
lutionary process. The tree can spare a
blossom better than a root. Therefore no
subject in human life was for Whitman out-

lawed from the realm of poetry. Similarly he denied any distinction of importance between body and soul, since their mutual dependence, so far as human life is concerned, is so close as to imply unity ; and he denied any distinction of shame between one function of the body and another, or between the exercise of one sense or another, and all the parts of the human anatomy he held to be equally decent, since the whole body must be in harmony with itself before the soul can properly dwell in it.

In this region of Whitman's doctrine his readers have found most offence. Making all allowance for his theories, they feel here that he shows some fundamental lack of fineness. Obviously his sincere willingness to push a truth to its conclusion is greater than his good taste. Yet it has been observed that he offends only against the taste of social convention ; he is altogether proper if we allow him the scientific attitude of the surgeon or the biologist. Perhaps even this defence, however, does him injustice, for with all his science, he is not a dissector but a poet. He believes that life, at least in its highway, is forever ascending ; to be one with the ultimate good, man has but to live in that highway. There surely will be found all the elemental passions and capacities of life ; should we distrust or condemn anything found there ? Whatever in this highway is livable is good, thinks Whitman ; and he is bold indeed who at any point in evolution would say once for all what is evil and what is good. That this doctrine aims at the root of much conventional decency and morality is undeniable, yet the shock it gives us in Whitman is more of taste than of thought ; for we escape unshocked from the same potential ideas in Emerson's *Compensation* and in Hawthorne's *Scarlet Letter*.

After dwelling upon this aspect of Whitman, it is hardly necessary to say that his approach to truth is secular, as Emerson's is religious ; science for Whitman is what theology is for Emerson, who, though he learned from science, learned only what could be turned to moral or poetical account. But Whitman caught the relentless spirit of science, that will see into the remotest conclusions of the phenomenon, and he revelled in this spirit as a truth-lover must. Emerson's religion, more orthodox religion, his own science, another man's ignorance—all these were to him facts of life, as interesting as any other facts, and similarly fit for enthusiastic contemplation. He liked his science, but he also liked Emerson's religion. He did not care to decide whether to be a materialist or an idealist ; he preferred to be both. Only one idea he refused to entertain—the idea of death. In his position he was consciously logical; for he had set the standard of all things in the stream of life, and if this stream should for any one cease, what would become of that person's standards? Or from another angle, if the soul is eternal, there is no death; and if matter is eternal, if there is nothing else in the universe, if even consciousness is material, how can we be more dead than we are now?

"There is really no death;
And if ever there was, it led forward life, and does not
 wait at the end to arrest it,
And ceas'd the moment life appear'd.
All goes onward and outward—nothing collapses;
And to die is different from what any one supposed, and
 luckier.
Has any one supposed it lucky to be born
I hasten to inform him or her, it is just as lucky to die,
 and I know it."

If Whitman differs from Emerson in his passion for society and for all the communal interests of man, he again resembles him in his wariness of the past. His caution is far more obvious, however, in his manner than in his ideas, for his robust faith in the new day brushed easily aside those cobweb bonds of the ancestors from which Emerson extricated himself only with much finesse. It was rather in the language of his poetry that Whitman was on his guard against the past. In this point of view he has been much mis-

understood. He loved the classics of poetry,
and had no reform to make in any past age.
He did not, like Wordsworth, crusade against
artificial diction, nor did he propose for himself any diction notably simple or natural ;
his lines are full of unusual words, even words
from other languages. But he did intend, for
the greater clearness of his message, that his
language and his diction should connote no
other literature, no other epoch, than that
in which his subject at the moment belonged.
All poetic diction takes to itself through continued use certain suggestions or overtones,
and that writer would be maladroit who
expressed an idea in diction of a contrary suggestion. The diction of Keats does not fit
Mr. Kipling's ballads, nor would the diction
of those ballads, now that we are familiar
with them, serve easily for a different type of
subject. Poetic images also—the rose, the
stars, the moonlight—through long use have
been burdened with certain suggestions not to
be disregarded by the poet who uses them ;
they help him if they are what he wishes to
say, but they contradict him if he has a different intention. And rhythms are equally
bound up with moods and ideas. Who can
be bacchanalian in a hymn metre ?

Whitman wished to express the prospect
of science, the prospect of democracy, the
future of man. He wished his verse to sug-

gest novelty, to give no echo of any other age, not because he disliked the other ages, but because he did not happen to be living in them. He therefore framed his rhythms on the model of the recitative in the opera ; he made the rhythmic scheme conform frankly to the thought. It may be that his love of Ossian or of the Psalms may have suggested his grand rhythms rolling freely between prose and verse ; but he preferred to justify himself, with that prophetic sympathy that he often showed, by the development of music out of formal periods into free rhythms. Had he heard the most modern opera or seen the most modern paintings, he would have realized the fairness of his prophecy. He has been justified also by the failure of his imitators. To write formless lines does not assure such effects as he gets, not even if the result is like nothing that ever was before in poetry. What makes his rhythms so wonderful is that they do convey the American spirit, the exhilaration and the rush of life, the power, and also the lack of proportion. The expression is superlatively honest. He never spoiled a true idea in order to cramp it into a preconceived line or stanza. If he needed further justification, he seems to be getting it unexpectedly in our day from the theory of æsthetics propounded with much fascination by Benedetto Croce—a theory which makes all artistic form implicit in the idea. That Whitman was assured of his place in a future stage of thought and art is clear in many a curious passage. " You who celebrate bygones," he says to the historians, " I project the history of the future " ; and in the most explicit passage :

" Poets to come ! orators, singers, musicians to come
  Not to-day is to justify me, and answer what I am for ;
  But you, a new brood, native, athletic, continental,
    greater than before known,
  Arouse ! Arouse !—for you must justify me—you must
    answer.
  I myself but write one or two indicative words for the
    future,
  I but advance a moment, only to wheel and hurry back
    in the darkness.
  I am a man who, sauntering along, without fully stop-
    ping, turns a casual look upon you, and then averts
    his face,
  Leaving it to you to prove and define it,
  Expecting the main things from you."

Evidently Whitman was in the highest degree a theorizer about life and art. To prove his point he sometimes pressed it too far, as many another enthusiast has done. But it is altogether to his credit that his enthusiasms led consistently to the central interests of life, rather than to the outer marshes of fanaticism. The civil war put him and his theories to the test, and revealed both at their noblest. How broad his sympathies were is shown by contrast with the nobly imaginative but partisan war lyrics of Henry Howard Brownell (1820-1872). Whitman was a true patriot, loving the soil with all but religious fervour, and his theory made him a hater of slavery. He had, however, a more just sense of the importance of the slave question and the war than many of his contemporaries, and wherever he touches the subject he rises to a high seriousness which permits none of his usual lapses of taste. In much of his other work he had been illustrating a hobby, and at times we must forgive him, as for similar reasons we sometimes must forgive Wordsworth. But in all the poems dealing with the war he lost himself in the great moment. The significance which he attached to slavery is shown in " *I sing the body electric,*" first published in 1855. He describes a man's body at auction, and chides the auctioneer for missing the chief values of that body, for which " the globe lay preparing quintillions of years, without one animal or plant " ; and " the revolving cycles truly and steadily rolled." This is not only one man, he says ; this is the father of those who shall be fathers in their turns. " How do you know who shall come from the offspring of his offspring through the centuries ? Who might you find you have come from yourself if you could trace back through the centuries ? " Whitman never lost this grip on the significance of the crisis ; it is stated with haunting picturesqueness in *Ethiopia saluting the colours*, and in many another poem. The war songs are full of it, even when he turns aside for the moment to fix the memory of the cavalry crossing the ford, a superb war picture, or more powerfully to record the heroic agonies and comfortings he witnessed among the wounded. To see what new poetry America through him was giving the world, we have but to compare the lost battlefield in Tennyson's *Passing of Arthur* with such poems as *A sight in the camp in the daybreak, Vigil strange I kept,* and *Look down, fair moon.* But even from such pictures Whitman recurs to the central idea of the significance of the war, and the climax of all these poems is the *Spirit whose work is done,* in which he prays that the majestic battle spirit may be eternal in his songs.

Against this epic conception of the war the two great poems on Lincoln stand out, the finest of American elegies. *Captain, My Captain* is naturally better known, for it has the advantage of conciseness and vivid feeling, but *When lilacs last in the dooryard bloomed* is equally interesting in other ways, perhaps for a different audience. Whitman summons in it his generous philosophy of life to comfort him in a personal grief, where

P

in the other poem he was only stating that grief. Both elegies are more full of echoes than he usually permits his work to be, but the subject was not one of novelty in man's long record.

Apart from the war poems, in which the subject was given to him by fate, it needs no argument to suggest that Whitman's genius would naturally express itself in celebration of nature in her larger aspects. No poetic medium could be imagined better fitted to deal with prairies and rough mountain country and uncouth towns than his all-but-formless rhythms. He differs from other nature-lovers in American or perhaps any other literature, in that he seems to have loved all portions of nature equally. He liked the mountains and the sea, but he did not prefer them to the inland plains. He found his joy in the cities as well as in the woods. At least he tried to love nature without distinction. But his happiest nature poems, in the opinion of most of his readers, describe the sea. *Out of the cradle endlessly rocking*, and the other poems entitled *Sea Shore Memories*, and the many poems of the soul in which the sea occurs as an image, make up a group that is obscured in Whitman's total work only because his best is so fine.

Whitman cannot be fully understood without an acquaintance with his prose, which reveals a character consistent with the noblest of the poetry, and sometimes, as in his record of his war experiences, a character even nobler than his best poem. It is probably too early to judge a man whose work, as he knew, was prophetic. How far his life conditioned his philosophy or his philosophy his conduct, no one can say. It appears, however, that time is dealing kindly with all sides of his reputation. Some things that he accomplished for American poetry are already fairly clear; he is the bard of industry, energy, and power; on his cruder side he has been said to be the mouthpiece of that strenuousness which for many Americans has been an attractive ideal. More nobly, he voices the hope of the lower classes, the emigrant hope, of the United States; he sings of democracy as a means of rescue for all fallen men; he is always bidding man stand upright. And in his view of life he is the largest account that America has given of herself to the world; she has not yet grown up to his vague but gorgeous dreams of her. In the old world, too, he has had a career; no revolution that purposes to better human conditions is likely to fail of finding its text in him. But with that reform which proposes an immediate end he has little in common; the truth of life, for him as for Emerson, is strictly, mathematically, in infinites.

" This day before dawn I ascended a hill, and look'd at
    the crowded heaven,
And I said to my Spirit, *When we become the enfolders*
    of those orbs, and the pleasure and knowledge of
    everything in them, shall we be filled and satisfied then ?
And my Spirit said, *No, we but level that lift to pass and*
    continue beyond."

Whitman's genius was helped rather than
hindered by the war; but if that terrible
struggle furnished his titan soul with inspiration, it also overwhelmed many a more refined and sensitive spirit. Certainly it crip-
pled the work of Paul Hamilton Hayne
(1830-1886), and literally shortened the life of
Henry Timrod (1829-1869). These two brilliant friends, both born in Charleston, South
Carolina, are still the best remembered of
the young admirers and followers of Simms.
Like him they held to the politer traditions of
English poetry; in their verse the courtly
graces of the fated social order which they
represented had almost its last expression.

In the north the chief poetic reputation
after the war was that of the Pennsylvanian,
Bayard Taylor (1825-1878), who, though he
began to publish verse in 1844, was princi-
pally known as a traveller and writer upon
travel, until 1870 and 1871, when the two
parts of his fine translation of *Faust* were
published. This is still the best poetic translation that has been made by an American,

not excepting Bryant's Homer and Longfellow's Dante ; and though some of Taylor's
oriental lyrics, such as the familiar *From the
desert I come to thee*, have kept their popularity in musical settings, it is on the
Faust that his fame rests. In recognition
of his achievement he was made Minister
to Germany in February, 1878, but died
suddenly in Berlin in December of that
year.

A far more original poet than Taylor was
his friend Sidney Lanier (1842-1881). Born
in Georgia, Lanier had discovered his genius
for music, had been graduated from Ogle-
thorpe College and was teaching in that institution, before the war broke out. He took
an active part on the Southern side, and was
captured and imprisoned. When he was
released at the end of the war, his sufferings had
ruined his health, and he soon found himself
a hopeless consumptive. It was after he
realized that he could only postpone the end
that he made his reputation as poet and critic,
with a volume of verse in 1877, *The Science
of English Verse*, 1880, and a series of lectures
on the English novel published posthumously
in 1883. His musical and literary work was
done chiefly in Baltimore, where he played
the flute in the Peabody Symphony Concerts,
gave lectures to private classes, and lectured
before the Johns Hopkins University ; but

he made visits to the North, and was obliged to travel in the South and West in search of health. He died in North Carolina.

His poetry takes its quality from his knowledge of music and from his theories of the intimate relation of the two arts. Perhaps it would be accurate to speak of him as practising three arts, for his verse abounds in colour, and he puts the painter's eye and the musician's ear at the service of poetry. His longer poems, such as *Sunrise*, *The Marshes of Glynn*, and *Corn*, suggest in their stately development the symphony or the sonata. His fame, however, is confined more and more to a few affectionately remembered short pieces, notably the *Ballad of Trees* and *The Master*.

Of later poets it would be difficult to choose among Edward Rowland Sill (1841-1887) and four recently dead—Edmund Clarence Stedman, Thomas Bailey Aldrich, John Banister Tabb, and Richard Watson Gilder. Sill's work was at times imaginative and large ; Stedman was a sort of patriot of poetry, serving with his own lyrics and his criticisms and his anthologies all the causes of the muse ; Aldrich and Tabb were such masters of technique as America has not produced since Poe ; Gilder made his sincere and simple lyric gift count powerfully for the public good. If this survey of American verse must pause with them, and if no final judgment of them is yet possible, they at least show how high and untarnished the democracy holds the poetic ideals bequeathed to it

CHAPTER XII

AMERICAN literature has had a sort of frontier throughout the nineteenth century, in which a rough kind of humour has flourished. Other qualities also have distinguished it; it has been an interesting if not highly artistic record of the oddities turned up by a rapidly moving civilization; it has preserved especially that cheerful optimism which conditions and results from such rapid progress. This type of book on the borderland of American literature is illustrated by Augustus Baldwin Longstreet's *Georgia Scenes*, 1840; William Tappan Thompson's *Major Jones' Courtship*, 1840, a similar book of broad humour, also by a Georgian; Johnson Jones Hooper's *Adventures of Captain Simon Suggs*, 1846; and Joseph Glover Baldwin's *Flush Times of Alabama and Mississippi*. These examples all have to do with the South and Southwest; the West was made similarly the subject of humour by Captain George Horatio Derby—" John Phœnix "—a Massachusetts man who

232

had explored the West. His sketches were published in 1855 under the title of *Phœnixiana*. All this body of writing disappeared, properly enough, after it had served its ephemeral purpose, but it is still important as the background of American humour to-day. Especially does it serve as an introduction to Bret Harte and to Mark Twain, whose superior genius supplanted it and helped to render it forgotten.

Francis Bret Harte was born in Albany, New York, on August 25, 1839. His father was teacher of Greek in a local seminary; of his mother's temperament and tastes we know that she was enterprising enough to accompany her son later to California. Of his ancestry further it is enough to say that he was of English, German, and Hebrew blood, and that his father was a Roman Catholic and his mother a Protestant. His Americanism is chiefly in his writings. His boyhood was of a piece with his later life, somewhat aimless. His health was not good, and he used that fact to escape much regular study, but he read the standard novelists and fell in love with Dickens.

In 1856 he went with his mother to California. It is not clear why he went, unless the general quest for gold in the new country may be taken as reason enough; if that was his motive he certainly soon recovered from any intention of being a miner—or perhaps he had persuasions now unknown for trying other careers. He was successively an express company messenger, a drug clerk, a printer, a school teacher, and an Indian fighter. In none of these functions did he achieve financial success, yet he seems to have given up each under some form of compulsion. The drug business ceased to be interesting after he had nearly killed a patient by a mistake in making-up a prescription, and the school had to be closed because most of the children moved away. If this record of his California beginnings seems discreditable, perhaps we should remember that he tells it himself, and he may have stretched a point or two at his own expense for the story's sake.

His permanent success began in 1862, when he was appointed secretary to the Superintendent of the Mint in San Francisco. In this year also he had married Miss Anna Griswold, and the miscellaneous writing that had made him known in the local papers already encouraged him to think of a literary career. So much did he think of it that his position in the Mint must have been a sinecure. It was during this period of established leisure that he published his *Condensed Novels* in *The Golden Era*, and made friends of Mark Twain, of Charles Webb, who owned and edited *The Californian*, founded in 1864,

and of Charles Warren Stoddard, the author
of *South Sea Idyls*. He also edited a collection of Western verse, which he has immor-
talized in his account of his critics in *My
First Book*. In 1865 he published a volume
of his own verse, *The Lost Galleon*. His
reputation grew so rapidly, in a community
where any great literary skill would have
few rivals, that in 1868, when Anton Roman,
a San Francisco bookseller and publisher,
founded a new magazine called *The Overland Monthly*, Bret Harte became its editor.
To its first number, in July, he contributed
a poem ; in the second number he printed
The Luck of Roaring Camp.

His account of the difficulties of getting
this famous story through his own press is
in itself a commentary on some contested
points of his reputation. Many a loyal
Californian has insisted that such a picture
as is given in *The Luck of Roaring Camp* is
untrue ; however alluring the picture, California was never so primitive nor so uncon-
ventional. These protests usually have come
from San Franciscans, whose natural pride
in their city made them frown on anything
less respectable and proper than the Eastern
civilization would admit. Indeed, the Western city, true to the common behaviour of
provincialism, was far stricter in its propriety
than the East. Bret Harte's story of the

mining camp, therefore, shocked his associates on *The Overland Monthly*. The publisher in dismay and anxiety notified him that in the printer's opinion the story was "indecent, irreligious, and improper," and that the proof-reader—a young lady—" had with difficulty been induced to continue its perusal." Bret Harte insisted, however, on printing the story as he had written it, and the publisher consented rather than accept the editor's resignation, which was the alternative. When the story appeared, "the secular press," the author tells us, "received it coldly and referred to its ' singularity '; the religious press frantically excommunicated it, and anathematized it as the offspring of evil ; the high promise of *The Overland Monthly* was said to have been ruined by its birth ; Christians were cautioned against pollution by its contact ; practical business men were gravely urged to condemn and frown upon this picture of Californian society that was not conducive to Eastern immigration ; its hapless author was held up to obloquy as a man who had abused a sacred trust."

The local criticism suffered a dramatic rebuke when the first mail from the East brought a letter from *The Atlantic Monthly*, requesting the delighted author to furnish that periodical with more stories like *The Luck of Roaring Camp*. Within a year he wrote and published *The Outcasts of Poker Flat*, *Tennessee's Partner*, and other well-known tales, and collected them all in a volume called *The Luck of Roaring Camp and other Sketches.* His growing reputation came to its first climax in 1870, when *The Heathen Chinee* appeared in his magazine. For this clever piece he never cared greatly ; he had written it for the sake of burlesquing the metre of the antiphonal dirge at the end of Swinburne's *Atalanta in Calydon.* But his Eastern readers placed a higher value on the poem, and their applause was equivalent to an invitation to return to his own part of the country. He therefore recrossed the continent in 1871, in a sort of triumphal progress, and with his attractive manners and handsome appearance he justified the romantic notion of him that his readers had formed. For the moment he became a sort of national hero, and the critics in France, England, and Germany read and approved his stories with less condescension than they usually had for new American authors.

There can hardly be two opinions as to Bret Harte's mistake in leaving the West. The older part of the country had nothing to give him but flattery, and that his nature was better without. He seems not to have realized that his genius was limited to the Western scene ; when he ventured into other phases of life, as in *Thankful Blossom*, he failed. Something in the eventful, irresponsible world of the forty-niners, which he knew or thought he knew, called out his ability by a magic summons. Anything worth while that he wrote after coming East was drawn from the stock of old memories; he could say nothing new.

The praise that welcomed him he mistook for prosperity. A spirit less steady might have been dazzled by such prospects. He was invited to dramatize his stories, he was retained to write for magazines, he was encouraged to submit new books to the publishers; and he felt safe, apparently, in living beyond his means and almost up to his prospects. He made his home in New York at first, later in Morristown, New Jersey, but his summers he passed at expensive places, like Newport or Lenox; and meanwhile the quality of his work fell off; his dramatization for Stuart Robson was a failure, his long novel, *Gabriel Conroy*, was uninteresting, and the hoped-for contributions to the magazines did not get written. At least the stories of him that linger in the old magazine offices are all in one tone of disappointed hope. His memory has had its loyal defenders; some of his friends have tried to prove that he did settle his bills and conduct his affairs efficiently. But after an attempt at lecturing, which succeeded only at first, he was glad to turn to a government post at Crefeld, Prussia.

He never saw his country again—not that his duties abroad proved interesting or confining, but because he had become hopelessly unsettled. He found his work at Crefeld irksome, and spent much of his time visiting in England, where he had many friends. At first he was received as a literary lion; then he attempted to turn his popularity into cash by a lecturing tour, and on this footing found the English less hospitable. A second similar attempt proved more remunerative, but on the whole England, like the Eastern part of America, grew tired of him. As he stayed in England, however, the largest part of his time, his government seems to have had so keen a sense of humour as to transfer him to a post from which at least he would not be absent so far, and in 1880 he was made consul at Glasgow. He liked to tell how, when his inquisitive Scotch landlady looked over his luggage, she sternly asked where was his Bible. But she probably held few conversations with him. After five years of good company in England and considerable contribution to the American magazines, Bret Harte was removed by the Washington authorities, who had the impression that he neglected his duties. His life

continued much as before, until he died, on
May 5, 1902, in the home of one of his friends
at Camberley, Surrey.

The tragic decline of Bret Harte's character has affected his reputation at home
less than might have been expected of a
country that makes Poe's writings bear the
blame of his conduct. One explanation is
that Bret Harte's failings were not so well
known ; but a deeper reason is that his best
work lay in an ungoverned region of society,
and some wildness in his reputation would
seem to be a mere dressing of the part. The
world of the miners, in which floods and explo-
sions and snow storms claim victims at any
moment, or reckless shootings and well-meant
but sometimes mistaken hangings have a
depopulating effect so normal as to imply a
law of nature,—this world of luck was so
perfect a field for Bret Harte's gifts, that there
will always be some sympathy with those
who from the first claimed that his gifts
invented the field. He was sentimental and
melodramatic, and he could unfold a situation
better than he could solve it ; he usually
needs a convulsion of nature to end his stories.
The reason for his failure in subjects from
normal life is therefore obvious, and equally
clear is the cause of his success in a world
where convulsions of nature happen every
day. Accident was a normal, even inevitable,

thing in the mining camp and the frontier towns ; when he uses good or bad fortune to solve his problems, the effect is as though he were straining for realism. The sentimentality also, which would be rather watery in a representation of humdrum existence, is necessary in such stern crises as his Western stories are built on ; experience so grim develops sentimentality to make it livable. Where Bret Harte stepped out of this subject matter, however, he seemed but a poor imitator of Dickens.

Because the typical subject of his stories is laid in such a world of accident, it is comparatively easy for Bret Harte to transcribe actual occurrences ; for the difference between a " true story " and a story acceptable as art is usually that art demands a reasoned solution, an intelligent ordering of what were crude facts. But where truth to life demands a departure from this kind of art, the writer can safely do without the mathematical conscience of a Poe, or the moral justice of a Hawthorne, and still seem true ; for whatever happens will have in it a sort of fatalism superior to literary craft. *Tennessee's Partner* is a true story, and it has the utmost of the unexpected and the accidental ; yet it is full of fate also, and few of Bret Harte's tales are so finely sentimental.

If Bret Harte had to make little change

Q

in the real incident to make it serve as a
plot, he was also fortunate in having characters ready to his hand. Even more than
the frontier of Cooper, the mining camp was
a sieve as well as a sink of personalities, and
the residuum was as strong and well-defined
as could be wished. The men were all cool,
resourceful, and fatalistic—so much uni-
formity their life forced upon them; but in
other respects they developed extravagant
forms of personality. Good and bad were
mixed; they came from the ends of the earth,
every man with his own secret, which it
was not good form to enquire into; and each
within his own character was a paradox.
"The greatest scamp had a Raphael face,
with a profusion of blonde hair; Oakhurst,
a gambler, had the melancholy air and intellectual abstraction of a Hamlet; the coolest
and most courageous man was scarcely over
five feet in height, with a soft voice and an
embarrassed, timid manner. The term
'roughs' applied to them was a distinction
rather than a definition. Perhaps in the
minor details of fingers, toes, ears, etc., the
camp may have been deficient, but these
slight omissions did not detract from their
aggregate force. The strongest man had but
three fingers on his right hand; the best
shot had but one eye."

It is obvious that a world of such incon-

gruities will furnish inspiration to the humorist, and Bret Harte's reputation is best sub-
stantiated by his humour. Whatever his
craft of plot-making might lack, he had the
eye and the heart for all humorous possibilities. His fun is of a more restrained
kind than most American joking; he has
been eclipsed among general readers by
Mark Twain, for example, whose force is
often greater but his delicacy much less.
Harte was willing to leave humour where he
found it, in its natural setting of life, part of
the characters, not greatly magnified or
relieved by exaggeration. In spite of his
very local subjects, in his fine restraint he
often seems closer to the English humorists
than to any of his countrymen. The opening
of *Mr. Thompson's Prodigal* illustrates this
quality. "We all knew that Mr. Thompson
was looking for his son, and a pretty bad one
at that. That he was coming to California
for this sole object was no secret to his fellow-
passengers; and the physical peculiarities
as well as moral weaknesses of the missing
prodigal were made equally plain to us through
the frank volubility of the parent. 'You was
speaking of a young man which was hung at
Red Dog for sluice-robbing,' said Mr. Thompson to a steerage passenger one day; 'be you
aware of the colour of his eyes?' 'Black,'
responded the passenger. 'Ah!' said Mr.

Thompson, referring to some mental memoranda, ' Charles's eyes was blue.' "[1]

But it is convenient here to pass from Bret Harte to Samuel Langhorne Clemens, whom Americans always speak of as Mark Twain. His death at a good age is so recent that no summary valuation of his work is likely to be satisfactory, and still less any detailed comparison of his position in latter-day American literature with that attained by some of his eminent contemporaries still fortunately living, like Mr. Howells and Mr. Henry James. His humour had its roots in the same rough frontier of literature as Bret Harte's, and he never allowed its original sturdiness or violence to be much toned down. He seems to foreign countries to represent the typical American humour, because in much of his work he delights in extravagant contrasts, exaggerations, and absurdities ; and that sort of taste is to be expected of a wild country. The foreign

[1] If space permitted, an adequate record should be made of the further literary history of the South and West. Of late years a large number of writers have caught and preserved vanishing phases of Southern life ; not the least loved of these authors is the late Joel Chandler Harris, whose stories of negro folklore have become almost household classics in the United States. Were not Mr. George W. Cable still fortunately among us, an extended reckoning would have to be made of his charming stories of Creole ife in New Orleans.

opinion of American humour was correct when it was first formed, seventy-five years ago ; it was correct when Artemus Ward (Charles Farrar Browne) made London laugh, and it was correct when Mark Twain began to delight his countrymen with the story of the Jumping Frog—the story which he recited to Bret Harte. But of late decades it has been pathetically clear that Americans have developed past their taste for Mark Twain's type of fun-making ; and if they have remained his ardent and grateful admirers in spite of that change, the tribute has been rather to his manly character than to his writing.

He was born in humble circumstances in Florida, Missouri, November 30, 1835. From his father, who combined a law practice with trade, he is thought to have inherited those visionary tendencies which he represented in his famous Colonel Mulberry Sellars. In Hannibal, Missouri, where the family were already living when the father died in 1847, Mark Twain began his varied career with some newspaper writing. A few years later he was working as a printer in New York, and later in Philadelphia. Returning to the Mississippi Valley he determined to be a river pilot, and after earning the necessary fee for instruction, in less than two years he qualified with sufficient skill to navigate between New Orleans and St. Louis. This part of his life he has told in *Life on the Mississippi*, 1883.

After a brief service in the Confederate army under General Sterling Price, Mark Twain went to Nevada, where a brother of his was Secretary of the Territory. Here in 1862 he began to write articles under the penname by which he is now known, and republished them in the Virginia City *Enterprise*. Appreciative members of the editorial staff encouraged his singular gifts of drollery, and in 1865 he was invited to a position on the San Francisco *Call*. He made the change, and soon found himself launched on his literary success. He collected his *Jumping Frog* and other newspaper sketches, in 1867, and the reputation they got for him caused several newspapers to send him abroad with a party of tourists, that he might report the trip humorously. The result was *The Innocents Abroad*, 1869, which firmly established his American fame. This volume may well be taken as the last successful example of the old extravagant American humour.

In 1870 Mark Twain married Miss Olivia Langdon, of Elmira, New York, and settled for a while in Buffalo, then for many years in Hartford. He published volumes at frequent intervals, which for the most part were in the old extravagant vein and have already been forgotten. But in 1876, with

The Adventures of Tom Sawyer, began that all too brief series of American scenes, of which the other books are *The Adventures of Huckleberry Finn,* 1885 ; *Pudd'nhead Wilson,* 1894 ; and *The Man that Corrupted Hadleyburg,* 1900. The first of these won him his reputation in England, where *The Innocents Abroad* could hardly be appreciated. To value any of these later stories at their true greatness, the critic must consider their author as something far more than a funmaker.

Long before this series was finished, however, Mark Twain had suffered that severe financial loss which served to reveal his strength of character. He had invested heavily in a publishing house which in 1894 failed for a large sum of money. This he assumed as a personal debt. The old-fashioned sense of honour which prompted his resolution to make a lecture tour of the world, and the courage with which he carried out the plan, are the chief causes why he is so dearly loved by Americans. Bret Harte disappointed his countrymen, but Mark Twain was a large asset of national pride. It naturally took nothing from the merit of his action that he thoroughly disliked lecturing, and before his losses he had resolved never to lecture again. His trip around the world was a delight to his audiences. Who that ever heard him can forget his unique drollery ! When he returned his debts were paid.

His later years were filled with public honour and private sorrow. The deaths of two daughters and of his wife almost unsettled his faith in any comfort or profit in this world or another. Even before these griefs the tragic note had been struck in *Pudd'n-head Wilson*, and his story of Hadleyburg was cynically wise. In his lesser writing during these years he often forced the note of humour back into his old extravagances, and where they could not laugh, his affectionate readers admired the courage that so tried to conceal a sad heart. He died at his home in Redding, Connecticut, on April 21, 1910.

Mark Twain is more certain of remembrance as a novelist than as a humorist. With changes of culture and taste his humour —at least many portions of it—will probably recede beyond general appreciation. Had he no other qualities, he might even now begin to take his place with the jokers out of fashion, like Josh Billings or Artemus Ward. But beginning with *The Adventures of Tom Sawyer* he showed himself to be a novelist of the first rank, a painter of manners and customs, a remarkable analyser of character, a master of dramatic plot. That book proved his phenomenal understanding

of the American small boy, and of those
aspects of human nature which expand in
the small, wide-settled villages of inland
America. The tramp, the loafer, the peddler,
all the local characters that might have
significance in the eyes of the small boy, are
represented with fascinating realism, as well
as the more respectable but less interesting
domestic characters—but all of them viewed
at all times through the eyes of the urchin.

Even in the story of *Tom Sawyer* Mark
Twain suggested a certain tragic contrast
between the boy's simple point of view and
the things that he saw but did not understand. In *The Adventures of Huckleberry
Finn* this note of elemental tragedy is increased until certain passages, such as the
relation of Huckleberry to his father, and
the episode of the Southern feud, would be
hard to overmatch in any literature. The
effect is to subdue the fun somewhat; the
book is not so popular as *Tom Sawyer* with
those who expect mere laughter from Mark
Twain. Still less fun is in *Pudd'nhead Wilson*.
If it were not for the quotations from *Pudd'n-
head's* diary, a laugh could hardly be found
in this grim drama of a slave-holding society.
It is the artistic version of that blot on the
American life which Mrs. Stowe discussed
more vividly and popularly in *Uncle Tom*.
But Mrs. Stowe had no such gifts for plot

as the man who invented this problem of the quadroon changeling in the white family who sells his old mother down the river that she may not betray his base birth.

The Man that Corrupted Hadleyburg is quite the keenest arraignment that American character has yet had. It would not lessen the bitterness of the satire were we to consider it directed not at one country but at human nature. And in any case the supposition cannot be made, for Mark Twain's ability to portray his countrymen so that they could recognize themselves improved every year of his life. This fine story, so bitter and so true, is evidence not only of disappointments that had taken away his joy in life, but also of that fine morality that cannot withhold contempt from the occasional vulgar meanness of democratic man.

That the best critical appraisers of America's virtues and failings should be found among the most distinctively national and loyal of her sons, such as Lowell and Mark Twain, is an augury for her ordered progress in all things, and an encouraging thought with which to close this brief record of her chief achievements in literature.

NOTE OF BOOKS

ADAMS, O. F., *Brief Handbook of American Literature* (1905).

American Men of Letters. Lives of Cooper (Lounsbury), Poe (Woodberry), etc.

BAKER, E. A., *Descriptive Guide to American Fiction* (1903).

BROWNELL, W. C., *American Prose Masters* (1910).

BURROUGHS, JOHN, *Whitman, a Study* (1896).

CARPENTER, G. R., *American Prose* (1898).

DUYCKINCK, E. A. and G. L., *Cyclopaedia of American Literature* (2 vols. 1855, 1875).

ERSKINE, JOHN, *Leading American Novelists* (1910).

GRISWOLD, W. M., *Directory of Writers* (1890); *Descriptive List of American Fiction* (2 vols. 1890, 1891).

HALE, E. E., *J. R. Lowell and His Friends* (1899).

HAWEIS, H. R., *American Humorists* (1883).

HIGGINSON, T. W., *Contemporaries ; Part of a Man's Life.*

HOWELLS, W. D., *Literary Friends and Acquaintances* (1901).

LAWTON, W. C., *New England Poets* (1898).

LINTON, W. J., *Poetry of America* (1776-1876); *An Anthology* (1878).

LOWELL, J. R., *Among My Books* (1882); *My Study Windows* (1891).

NICHOL, J., *American Literature, 1620-1880* (1882).

ONDERDONK, J. L. A., *History of American Verse* (1901).

251

PAYNE, W. M., *Leading American Essayists* (1910).

RICHARDSON, C. F., *American Literature*, 1607-1885, 2 vols. (1887).

STEDMAN, E. C., *Poets of America* (1885); *An American Anthology* (1900).

STEDMAN, E. C., and E. M. HUTCHINSON, *Library of American Literature* (11 vols., 1888-90).

STANTON, THEODORE, *A Manual of American Literature* (1909).

TRENT, W. P., *A History of American Literature* (1607-1865 (1903).

TRENT, W. P., and B. W. WELLS, *Colonial Prose and Poetry* (3 vols., 1901).

TYLER, M. C., *A History of American Literature during the Colonial Time* (2 vols., 1878); *The Literary History of the American Revolution* (2 vols., 1897).

WENDELL, B., *Literary History* (1901).

WHIPPLE, E. P., *American Literature* (1887).

INDEX